THE OLD CHURCH

Bry Cooper

Published in 2023 by Bryan Cooper

© Copyright Bryan Cooper

ISBN: 978-1-913898-73-1

Newspaper images ©The British Library Board. All rights reserved. With thanks to The British Newspaper Archive (www.britishnewspaper archive.co.uk)

Other photographs sourced/taken by the author/publisher Bryan Cooper and referenced accordingly throughout the book.
Every attempt has been made to contact copyright holders of material in this book where it was deemed necessary. However, if an omission has occurred future editions will include acknowledgments

A Catalogue record for this book is
available from the British Library.

Printed by IngramSpark

All rights reserved without limiting the rights under copyright reserved above, no parts of this publication may be reproduced, stored in or introduced into a retrieval system, or transmitted in any form, or by any means (electronic, mechanical, photocopying, recording or otherwise) without the prior written permission of Bryan Cooper, the copyright owner and the publisher of this book.

Front Cover: The Hudleston Chapel Holy Trinity Church, Millom

FOREWORD

The history of the Church of the Holy Trinity in Millom, affectionately known as the Old Church by many generations of the local inhabitants of the town where I spent my childhood, has been well documented over the years.

During my research into the history of Millom over the last 10 years or so, I have collected many snippets of information, not about the history, but many other interesting facts relating to the Church from the British Newspaper Archives, and these appear in chronological order within the pages of this book.

Most of the information, I believe, has never seen the light of day before and has mostly been penned by unnamed others and transcribed by me.

The images I have used are from a variety of sources including a few of my own, and again, some of which have never been seen before.

PAGE	CONTENTS
1	Index
4	Rev. Henry Pickthall presented to the Vicarage of Millom
	Richard Noble death
	Millom Church
5	Death of Rev. Henry Pickthall
	Rev. Edmund Edward Allen instituted to the vicarage of Millom
6	Polish exile Charles Stolzman
7	Re-pewing of Millom Parish Church
	Opening of Millom School
8	Millom Church restoration and the Vesica window
9	Re-opening of Millom Church following restoration
10	Donations towards Millom Church Restoration Fund
	Sermons preached on behalf of Church restoration and School building funds
	Final subscriptions for Millom Church restoration and Millom School
11	Re-opening of Millom Church organ
	Consecration of additional burial ground
	Millom School House
12	Rev. E. E. Allen departure
	Rev. J. Irving presented to the Vicarage of Millom
	Rev. E. E. Allen and Millom School
13	Rev. J. Irving marriage
	Presentation to Rev. J. Irving
14	Old Millom Vicarage for sale
	Millom Churchyard
	New Millom Vicarage
	A female Sexton
15	Foundation stone laid for new Millom Vicarage
	Presentation to the Reverend T. Hackworth
16	Restoration of the Old Church
	An amusing incident
	Gas supply for the Old Church
17	Thomas Whinnerah memorial window
18	Harvest thanksgiving service
19	Bazaar to raise funds for heating apparatus
	Illness of Rev. J. Irving
	Burial ground consecration
20	Millom Old Church
21	Stoney family tragedies
22	Death of Rev. E. E. Allen
23	Rev. E. E. Allen memorial windows
	Purchase of the Drill Hall
	Rev. H. Banks-Villiers accepts curacy at Holy Trinity
	Rev. W. S. Sykes accepts Vicarage of Eskdale
24	Presentation to Rev. W. S. Sykes
	Tragic death of Rev. H. Banks-Villiers
25	Death and funeral of Mrs. Irving, wife of Rev. J. Irving
26	Pickings from Millom Churchyard
28	Unveiling of memorial to George Mason Park
29	Testimonial to Rev. J. Irving

29	Presentation to Rev. J. Irving
	Rev. J. Irving falls in Church
30	Rev. G. Yorke presented to the Rectory of Bewcastle
	Rev. Davis accepts curacy of Holy Trinity
	Millom Parish Church Choir at Holy Trinity Vicarage
31	Juvenile crime in Holy Trinity Churchyard
	Church Institute at Millom
32	Millom Parish Church Institute. Grand bazaar in the Drill Hall
33	Death and funeral of Canon John Irving
36	Rev. Charles Whittaker acceptance and resignation
37	Rev. William Kewley appointed Vicar of Holy Trinity Church
39	Canon Irving memorial porch
40	Opening of Millom Parish Church Institute
42	Tragic death and following death inquest of Rev. William Kewley
45	Funeral of Rev. Wm. Kewley
46	The late Rev. Wm. Kewley memorial proposal
	Rev. R. S. G. Green appointed Vicar of Holy Trinity and Institution
47	Rev. R. S. G. Green Induction
48	Rev. J. Irving and Mrs. Irving memorial window
49	Rev. W. Kewley memorial tablet
	Millom Parish Church c.1909
50	Rev. J. H. Watson new curate of the Parish Church
	Rev. J. H. Watson death, death inquest and funeral
52	Ordination of Rev. George William Lemmon
	Rev. R. S. G. Green accepts living of Wetheral
	Rev. R. D. Ellwood accepts living of Holy Trinity parish
53	Roman coin find in Holy Trinity Churchyard
	Rev. R. D. Ellwood Institution and Induction
54	Flint scraper found at Millom Vicarage
	History of Millom Parish Church. A short sketch by Rev. R. D. Ellwood
55	Renovation of Millom Parish Church
	Interesting discovery at Millom Parish Church. Ancient piscina and credence shelf
	Rev. R. D. Ellwood's "History of Millom Parish Church" book released
56	Former Millom Vicar son's death tragedy
	Memorial organ for Parish Church
	Old Church tea party
57	Memorial organ and Church renovation fund
	Easter Vestries. Church renovation fund, the old sundial
58	A relic of bygone days. The old sundial
59	Dedication service for the old sundial
60	Louth Disaster Relief Fund
61	Faculty granted to move and install memorial tablets
62	Parishioners gift to Millom Vicar
63	Concert held in the Co-operative Hall in aid of Church restoration and organ fund
64	Rev. David Whiteley Irving new Vicar of Holy Trinity, Institution and Induction
65	Restoration of the Church or augmentation of the living
67	Unveiling and dedication of War Memorial tablet
69	Millom Parish Church garden fete in aid of the Parish Church restoration fund
70	The Parish Church restoration scheme
	Items of interest. Brief Church restoration details

71	Sale of Work at Millom Castle in aid of Church restoration fund
73	Millom facts and fancies
74	Sale of Work in the Drill Hall in aid of Church restoration fund
75	G.F.S. (Girl's Friendly Society) Sale of Work at Millom Castle
76	Millom Parish Church. A venerable pile of Saxon origin
78	Millom Parish Church restoration scheme. Scheme approved by Council
79	G.F.S. Oriental Bazaar in the Drill Hall in aid of Church restoration fund
80	Millom Church restoration scheme declined at Carlisle Consistory Court
80	Rev. D. W. Irving presented to the living at St. Stephen's, Carlisle
80	Petition to Bishop of Carlisle relating to the departure of Rev. D. W. Irving
81	Rev. D. W. Irving's departure from Millom
81	Vicar of Shap's appointment to Millom Parish Church
81	Presentation to Rev. D. W. Irving
83	Institution of the Rev. P. A. Stewart
83	Rev. P. A. Stewart marriage
83	Some notes on Millom Parish
84	Rev. P. A. Stewart resigns and accepts the living at Scotby
84	New Vicar for Millom. Rev. W. J. Phythian-Adams of St. Mary's, Wellingborough
85	Induction of former Millom Vicar Rev. R. D. Ellwood to St. Mary's, Carlisle
85	Death of William Henry Kitchin, Parish Clerk of Holy Trinity for 29 years
86	Holy Trinity Dedication festival
86	Gravedigger wanted for Millom Parish Church
86	Imperial War Graves Commission. Headstones erected at Holy Trinity
87	Pre-1930 plan of Holy Trinity Church seating plan
88	The Church of the Holy Trinity, Millom. The life story of a Holy place
94	Millom Church alterations
94	Faculty granted for reconstruction
94	The Old Parish Church. Correspondence from Rev. Phythian-Adams to The Millom Gazette
96	Church restoration. Before and after plans from a souvenir of the restoration
98	Who were they?
99	Millom Parish Church. First stages of restoration
101	The Chancel before and after restoration
102	Arthur Riding. Former local Licensee interred on 2 continents
103	Rev. W. J. Phythian Adams restoration notes in the Parish Church magazine
104	Historical event at Millom Parish Church. Re-opening and Dedication
109	Millom Vicar's Diocesan appointment
109	Praise for Millom Vicar
109	Rev. M. M. Barlow. New Vicar of Millom
110	Rev. M. M. Barlow Induction at Millom Parish Church
110	Rev. W. J. Phythian-Adams appointed Canon of Carlisle Cathedral
110	Grand Oriental Bazaar in the Palace, Millom in aid of the Church restoration fund
114	Former Millom Vicar accepts post as Chaplain at Haifa, Palestine
114	Former Millom Vicar appointed Chaplain to the King
114	Rev. M. M. Barlow accepts living of Corbridge on Tyne
114	Rev. Samuel Taylor, Vicar of Holy Innocents, Manchester accepts living of Millom
114	Former Holy Trinity curate's marriage
115	Marriage of Edward Barry Cooper and Gladys Waugh at Holy Trinity Church
115	Bryan Cooper Baptism at Holy Trinity Church

Newspaper images © The British Library Board. All rights reserved. With thanks to The British Newspaper Archive (www.britishnewspaperarchive.co.uk)

1836

APPOINTMENT

The Rev. H. Pickthall has been presented by Lord Holland, as Chancellor of the Duchy of Lancaster, to the Vicarage of Millom, vacant by the death of the Rev. Henry Dixon, B.D.

Carlisle Patriot – Saturday, July 16th 1836

1841

RICHARD NOBLE DEATH

At Holborn Hill, Millom, on Thursday, the 10th inst., Mr. Richard Noble, aged 83 years. The deceased was a respectable joiner and had been upward of 52 years clerk and organist of the parish church of that place, which offices he executed with credit until within a few weeks of his death. He was followed to his grave by ten of his children.

Westmorland Gazette and Kendal Advertiser – Saturday, January 30th 1841

MILLOM CHURCH

The church of Millom, dedicated to the Holy Trinity, is situated in the township of Millom Below, closely adjoining the castle. Indeed, so close is their proximity, that from some points of view they appear as one building; very nearly resembling, in this respect, not in grandeur, the castle and church of Lancaster. The church consists of a nave and chancel, a south aisle, and a modern porch on the same side. Two bells are hung in a turret at the western end. In the church-yard are the remains of a cross, the shaft of which bears four shields; those on the east and west sides are charged with the arms of Hudleston, on the north and south with – impaling Hudleston. This church is a venerable edifice; but it is to be lamented that some of its wardens have been so deeply imbued with the love of improvements, that they have left few of the old windows – their places being supplied with very un-ecclesiastical substitutes. The roof of the nave was open to the timber work but it is now concealed by a modern ceiling. The north door has been walled up; it is circular-headed, and has a niche over the arch. The pulpit and reading desk are placed along the north wall; both are of oak, but painted of a mahogany colour! The base appears to be of stone, and it was the opinion of that accomplished antiquary, Dr. Whittaker, that it is a portion of an ancient, stone pulpit. A gallery at the west end contains an organ. Below this is an octagonal stone font, ornamented with quatrefoils and a shield charged with the arms of Hudleston and a label. The south aisle, or at least a portion of it, appears to have been a chapel belonging to the Hudlestons, lords of Millom. It opens from the nave by four pointed arches, springing from many circular and octagonal piers. The roof of this part of the church, until of late years, was open to the timber work, under which a ceiling is now placed. At the western end is an oval shaped window, now walled up. A large decorated window of five lights nearly fills the east end; this has been most barbarously walled up from the bottom to the spring of the arch, and two sash windows inserted. Near this window is a piscina, which sanctions to opinion that the whole or part of the south aisle has been a chapel. This aisle was the burial-place of the Hudlestons, who for a period of about five centuries were lords of the seigniory. Here is an altar-tomb, ornamented with Gothic tracery and figures bearing shields of arms, on which recline the effigies of a knight and his lady, in alabaster, very much mutilated: the knight is in plate armour, his head resting on a helmet, and having a collar of S.S; the lady is dressed in a long gown and mantle, with a veil. They appear to have originally been painted and gilt, but the greater part has been rubbed off. Near the altar-tomb are the very mutilated remains of a knight, carved in wood, "apparently of the fourteenth century." A few years ago there was "a lion at his feet." The chancel is not ceiled; it has a pointed east window of three lights, a small circular one, a narrow window with a rounded head, and another of two lights, with trefoiled heads, under a square dripstone.

Cumberland Pacquet and Ware's Whitehaven Advertiser – Tuesday, October 5th 1841

1854

DEATH OF REV. HENRY PICKTHALL

On the 22nd inst., at the Vicarage, Millom, Cumberland, very suddenly, the Rev. Henry Pickthall, vicar aged 61

The Westmorland Gazette and Kendal Advertiser – Saturday, April 29th 1854

The grave of Rev. Henry Pickthall in Holy Trinity Churchyard

"SACRED TO THE MEMORY OF THE REVD. HENRY PICKTHALL, B.A. QUEEN'S COLLEGE OXFORD. EIGHTEEN YEARS VICAR OF THIS PARISH WHO DEPARTED THIS LIFE APRIL 22ND 1854 AGED 62 YEARS. ALSO OF MARY, WIDOW OF THE ABOVE AND DAUGHTER OF THE REVD. EDWARD VARDY OF MARKET HARBOROUGH WHO DEPARTED THIS LIFE MARCH 20TH 1865 AGED 80 YEARS."

ECCLESIASTICAL INTELLIGENCE

The vicarage of Millom, near Ravenglass, in the diocese of Chester, has become vacant by the death of the Rev. Henry Pickthall, M.A. (instituted 1836). The benefice is worth 200l. a year, and is in the gift of the Chancellor of the Duchy of Lancaster

London Evening Standard – May 5th 1854

LONSDALE NORTH OF THE SANDS

PREFERMENT

The Bishop of Chester has instituted the Rev. Edmund Edward Allen, M.A., to the vicarage of Millom, near Ravenglass, Cumberland, rendered vacant by the death of the Rev. Henry Pickthall, M.A., on the nomination of the Chancellor of the Duchy of Lancaster.

The Kendal Mercury – July 15th 1854

POLISH EXILE CHARLES STOLZMAN

At Haverigg, Millom, on the 18th, very suddenly, at the house of Mr. John Kirkby, Mr. Stolzman, aged 60 years.

The Kendal Mercury and Northern Advertiser – Saturday, September 23rd 1854

On the 18th September, died at Haverigg, Cumberland, Charles Stolzman, one of the members of the Polish Centralization. He was born at Warsaw in 1793. In 1809 he entered the army in the Grand Duchy of Warsaw, and followed the French in their retreat through Leipsic, going into exile in France. After the French war and the establishment of the kingdom of Poland, remaining an artillery-officer in the Polish army, he conspired in November 1830, with the Belvedere ensigns, took part in the rising of Warsaw, defended its entrenchments in October 1831, following the retreating army and Government, and promoted by General Bem for his gallant conduct to the rank of lieutenant colonel of artillery, went into exile – for the rest of his life. During the revolution, he had belonged to what may be called the revolutionary and patriotic party, to distinguish it from the diplomatic Czartoryski party, which depended altogether on foreign courts. In exile he joined his friend Lelevel, the historian, and the democratic opposition. In 1833 he conspired with Colonel Zaliwski, who went with a number of volunteers to Poland, to begin there a guerrilla warfare, while Germany was to be roused to arms by a rising in Frankfort. To support the latter, Stolzman went, with the Polish exiles who were settled at Dijon and Besancon, to Switzerland, where, the Frankfort movement failing, they were obliged to remain. In Switzerland he became acquainted and soon intimate with Mazzini, and joined him in the Savoy expedition, which was baffled by the treachery of General Ramorino. The consequence of this failure was the organization by Mazzini of the association of *Young Europe*; formed of the committees of Young Italy, Young Germany, Young Switzerland and Young Poland, of the last of which Stolzman was a leading member. This Young Europe was the germ of the Central European Committee, founded in 1850. But the time was not then ripe. The Polish Emigration itself needed a national democratic organization. This the Polish Democratic Society was the preparing, while the Polish Union, of which Lelevel was the head, was seeking to embrace larger masses of men than were at all likely to be fit for such a purpose. The Union however persisting, the society of Young Poland was merged in it. Meanwhile Stolzman and his companions, expelled from Switzerland and the Continent, came to England. Here he was chosen a member of the Polish Committee in England; and when General Dwernicki, the head of the committee, went over to the Czaroryski faction, and so occasioned a split in the body, Stolzman and those who remained faithful to the Union formed themselves into one of its *Communes*, and so worked till 1847, when Stolzman taking the initiative, they joined the Democratic Society, whose principles indeed they had always held. In 1844 Stolzman published a work on *Partisan Warfare*, which, extensively circulated in Poland, kept up the spirit of the people, showing them how to depend upon their own resources. It was in 1844 that his and Mazzini's letters were opened in the English Post office, by order of Graham and Aberdeen. When 1848 roused Europe, Stolzman endeavoured to revisit his native land, but was unable to pass the frontier, and returned to England sorrow-stricken and changed. His faith remained, but his strength was giving way. In 1852 he left London to reside at Brantwood. Soon after his health began to fail rapidly. In the last few months, under a complication of disorders, he had become a feeble old man. For the sake of sea-bathing, he went to a little place called Haverigg, near Broughton-in-Furness; he had just been elected to the Polish Central Democratic Committee, and was anxious to recover some strength for his work, and for the longed for return to Poland, if England should dare be wise enough to aid Poland to rise against Russia. On the 18th of September, he was taken with a paralytic fit, and in three hours was dead. One more of us out of the battle, under God's shield. We buried him in the little churchyard of Millom, under the shadow of Black Combe, within hearing of the sea. His comrades far away, one English mourner stood alone beside the old soldier's grave, and he can speak of him but with a full heart – a heart too full for many words. None was ever truer, maulier, kindlier, more soldierly, more patriotic, or more worthy of all honourable recollection than my ten-year's-friend – *Charles Stolzman. W.J.L. – 'C. Stolzman,' extracted from the 'English Republic,' a monthly publication printed and published at Coniston.*

The Kendal Mercury – October 28th 1854

1858

TO CONTRACTORS

Persons desirous to contract for the Re-Pewing of Millom Parish Church and for other repairs and alterations therein, are requested to send Tenders to the Vicar and Churchwardens.

Plans to be seen at Millom Vicarage, near Underhill Station

Soulby's Ulverston Advertiser and General Intelligencer – Thursday, September 2nd 1858

OPENING OF MILLOM SCHOOL

Millom School 2023. Image © Bry Cooper

Yesterday, the district of Millom was unusually peopled, numerous visitors having arrived therein, by early morning trains from Whitehaven and Furness, to be present at the opening of a new school, which has been erected in connexion with and adjoining Millom Church, by voluntary subscriptions on the part of the parishioners, aided by a government grant. The building consists of two spacious rooms on the ground floor, and is a neat stone edifice.

After inspecting the school, the visitors joined a large congregation of the inhabitants of that and neighbouring parishes, who had assembled in the church. Prayers having been read by the vicar, assisted by the Venerable Archdeacon Evans, an appropriate and very impressive sermon was preached by the Rev. John Allen, Archdeacon of Salop, from the 3rd and 4th verses of the 127th Psalm:- "Lo, children are an heritage of the Lord and fruit of the womb is his reward. As arrows are in the hand of a mighty man so are children of the youth." At the close of service a collection was made, which amounted to the handsome sum of £25 1s.

Upon leaving the church, the company reassembled in the schoolroom, where was spread an elegant *dejeuner*, provided by Mr. Newton, of Holborn Hill. The chair was occupied by the Rev. E. E. Allen, M.A, vicar of Millom, and the vice-chair by the Rev. R. G. Calthorp, M.A., incumbent of Irton. Amongst those present we also observed the Venerable Archdeacon Evans; Venerable Archdeacon Allen; Rev. J. Rawlinson, rector of Broughton; Rev. J. S. Pinthorn, incumbent of Eskdale; Rev. J. Stackhouse, incumbent of Thwaites; Mrs. Brockbank, Chapples; Mrs. Calthorp, Irton; J. B. Wilson, Esq., and Mrs. Wilson, Whitehaven; Mrs. And Miss Rawlinson, Duddon Grove; Mrs. Allen, Millom; John Grice, Esq., Bootle; J. S. Myers, Esq., Po House; Mr. Barrett, Coniston; Mr. Sykes, Salthouse; Mr. John Benn, Hestham, &c.

The Chairman having given the usual loyal toasts, gave "The Bishop and Clergy of the diocese," coupling with the toast the name of the Venerable Archdeacon Evans. The clergy of the diocese were signally blessed of God in having such a bishop at their head. (Applause.) The Bishop of Carlisle, previous to his attaining to his present high position had been a hard-working parish clergyman, and none knew better than he the wants and the capacities of a country district. (Hear, hear.)

Archdeacon Evans, in responding to the toast with which his name had been coupled, said he had felt very great pleasure in co-operating with the Bishop of Carlisle, who had always recommended to parishioners the importance of working harmoniously with their ministers in the great work of providing efficient educational means for the young, and in supporting schools of the description of that whose opening they were then celebrating. The Bishop, too, he knew to be strongly of opinion, in which he (the speaker) entirely concurred, that very great benefit was likely to result from parishioners aiding their minister in the surveillance of the parish schoolmaster.

The Chairman next proposed the health of the Venerable Archdeacon Allen, who, he said, was one of the hardest-working clergymen of the day, and who had risen to his present eminence in the church, not by family patronage, but solely by his exertions as a devoted Christian minister.

The Venerable Archdeacon Allen, in acknowledging the compliment, said his heart and hopes had always been with educational movements, and Government had thought proper to appoint him one of its chief inspectors of schools, an office, the duties of which it was always a pleasure to him to discharge. It was solely owing to his love of schools, that he was induced to come from Shrewsbury to preach to them that day and to be present at the opening of their school. He trusted that gratitude for the great interest which their minister took in their educational and spiritual welfare would be abundantly manifested by them in their endeavours to assist him and the schoolmaster. (Cheers.). The company then separated.

In the afternoon, the children of the district were treated to tea and buns in the school-room.

The Whitehaven News – Thursday, October 28th 1858

1859

INTERESTING ARCHITECTURAL DISCOVERY

The Vesica or Fish window at Holy Trinity Church. L/H image (date unknown) before the 1930 restoration from the archives of Millom Heritage & Arts Centre. R/H image 2023 © Bry Cooper

On Monday, the workmen at Millom Parish Church, under the direction and superintendence of the incumbent, removed the rough-cast and rubble within the pane work of the remarkable vesica or fish-shaped window, at the west-end of the aisle, with the view of ascertaining whether any indications of the original tracery of the window could be found. After some hours' careful work, the original tracery, almost perfect in form, was brought to light from the mass of rubbish under which it has probably lain hid for upwards of a century. It proves to be a very beautiful and remarkable specimen of the decorated order of architecture. Careful drawings were immediately taken by Mrs. Allen, Millom Vicarage, and the Rev. G. Stanley Pinhorn, minister of Eskdale, as the old tracery, though almost perfect in form, is in parts crumbling and liable to fall to pieces. Antiquarians will find that a visit to this venerable church will not be unworthy of their attention, whilst this interesting relic is to be seen in its original form. The incumbent has decided, with the aid of those who feel interested in this fine old church, to restore this remarkable window as nearly as possible to its original form.

Cumberland Pacquet and Ware's Whitehaven Advertiser – Tuesday, March 8th 1859

MILLOM

OPENING OF CHURCH AND ORGAN

On Sunday last, the fine old church of the Holy Trinity, Millom, was re-opened for divine service, after considerable repairs and restoration; amongst which we may more particularly specify, the restoration of the very remarkable vesica window and of two beautiful decorated windows in the aisle; the opening out of the fine old oak roofs of both nave and aisle; the restoration of the old early English north door; new pulpit and desk, of oak; new seating to nave and aisle; and removal of the old unsightly west gallery. The restoration of simple early English windows to the nave is in course of operation.

At the same time the New Organ, erected by Messrs. W. Wilkinson and Son of Kendal, was opened under the able hands of our respected organist and fellow townsman Mr. Robert Daniel.

This instrument which reflects very great credit on the builders, is admirably adapted to the size of the church and the requirements of the congregation and contains the following stops:- Open diapason; stop diapason; bass: stop diapason, treble; dulciana; principal; twelfth; fifteenth; also two-and-a-half octaves of pedals to manuals. The dulciana is a particularly sweet stop, and the tones of the whole are rich and effective. A part of the pipes employed in its construction are fine old pipes from the old organ by Langshaw of Lancaster, which formerly stood in this church. The action and mechanical movements are well and soundly constructed, simple in arrangement, and work well and easily. The organ is erected on the ground at the south-west corner of the aisle.

One of the very largest congregations that ever assembled in this fine old church was gathered from all parts of this and the neighbouring parishes, filling the church in all parts where available space could be found.

Prayers were read by the Vicar, the Rev. E. E. Allen, R D., and an able, earnest, and appropriate sermon was preached by the Rev. R. Gordon Calthorp, M.A., Incumbent of Irton and Drigg, from 1 Cor. xiv, 15., "What is then? I will pray with the understanding also: I will sing with the spirit and I will sing with the understanding also." Mr. Calthorp pointed out how music, both instrumental and vocal, had always borne a leading part in the public service of adoration of the church of God, under each dispensation, and in all ages; and dwelt forcibly on the right and worthy manner of fulfilling this solemn duty; concluding with an eloquent exhortation to those present to go on with their work which they had so worthily begun.

Soulby's Ulverston Advertiser and General Intelligencer – July 14th 1859

MILLOM CHURCH

The fine old church of the Holy Trinity, at Millom, was re-opened last Sunday. It had been thoroughly repaired and restored. All the "improvements" which senseless and tasteless churchwardens, for above a century, had effected, in order to disguise the beauty of the sacred edifice, have been removed. Among the restorations are the very remarkable vesica window, and two beautiful decorated windows in the aisle; the opening out of the fine old oak roofs of both nave and aisle; the restoration of the early English north door; new pulpit and desk, of oak; new seating to nave and aisle; and removal of the old unsightly west gallery.

The restoration of simple early English windows to the nave is in course of operation; at the same time, a new organ, built by Messrs. Wilkinson and Son, of Kendal, was opened.

The Preston Chronicle and Lancashire Advertiser – July 16th 1859

MILLOM CHURCH

The treasurer of Millom Church Restoration Fund gratefully acknowledges the following donations:- Sir Hedworth Williamson, Bart, £10; Captain Rawlinson, Duddon Hall, £10; the Earl of Lonsdale (conditionally, on £200 being raised), £10; the Countess of Zetland, £5; J. B. Wilson, Esq., Whitehaven, £2; J. P. Myers, Esq., Broughton, £5; and Bernard Gilpin, Esq., £1 1s. The exertions of the respected vicar have gained him the good opinion of all classes of his parishioners. His out-door duties are zealously and regularly attended to, and the restoration of the church is regarded with hopefulness both by pastor and people.

The Whitehaven News – July 21st 1859

1860

MILLOM PARISH CHURCH

On Sunday last, the Venerable Archdeacon Evans preached on behalf of the Church Restoration Fund from Ephesians iv. 24 – "And that ye put on the new man, which after God is created in righteousness and true holiness." After an able and striking exposition of the text (which was from the epistle of the morning), with a forcible exemplification of the things which must be cast off in order to the change therein spoken of, - as the awful sin of drunkenness, which is so fearful a reproach to our district, - the venerable archdeacon made an earnest appeal to the congregation on behalf of the good work of cleansing and maintaining in order the house of prayer, as no small point in our Christian welfare. The collection amounted to £5 14s. 8d. The afternoon collection for the School Building Fund amounted to £3. 16s. 9d. – not by any means large sums, considering the wealth and prosperity of this large parish.

The Ulverston Mirror and Furness Reflector – Saturday, October 20th 1860

1861

Final voluntary subscriptions to pay off the deficiency in the Millom Church Restoration and School Building Funds.

	£	s.	d.
By Collections in Millom Church, Oct. 14, after Sermons by the Venerable Archdeacon Evans, Incumbent	9	11	5
The Vicar	25	0	0
Mr. Wm. Sykes, Salthouse	3	0	0
Mr. J. S. Myers, Poo House	2	0	0
Mr. Geo. Benn, Hestholm	1	10	0
Mr. Wm. Stable, Moor	1	0	0
Mr. J. Hodgson, Millom Castle	1	0	0
Miss Postlethwaite and family, Low House	1	0	0
Subscriptions under £1	2	10	0

Leaving deficiency exceeding £55. Subscriptions will be gratefully received by the Vicar of Millom, and by Messrs. Grice and Co., Bootle.

Ulverston Mirror and Furness Reflector – April 20th 1861

MILLOM PARISH CHURCH.

Sunday, April 21st. Re-opening of the Organ with considerable addition. Sermons will be preached in the Morning by the Rev. R. Gwillym, M.A., Incumbent of Ulverston and Rural Dean; in the Afternoon by the Rev. R. G. Calthrop, M.A., Incumbent of Drigg and Irton, on behalf of the Organ Fund and Church and School Building Funds.

Mr. R. Daniel, Organist of the Parish Church, Ulverston, will preside at the Organ.

Service, Morning, 10 30; Evening, 3 30.

Ulverston Mirror and Furness Reflector – April 20th 1861

1862

CONSECRATION SERVICES

On Monday week the Bishop of Carlisle consecrated a piece of ground at the west end of Millom Church, being an addition to the present churchyard. The piece of ground is nearly quarter of an acre in extent. Part of it has been given by Lord Lonsdale, and part by the Rev. E. E. Allen, the vicar of the parish. The following clergymen and others were present:- The Rev. H. Gwillyn, Vicar of Ulverston and Rural Dean; the Rev. Chancellor Burton; Rev. G. Wilkinson, Incumbent of Whicham; Rev. G. Ormandy, Vicar if Whitbeck; Rev. Mr. Stackhouse, Vicar of Thwaites; Rev. R. G. Calthorp, Incumbent of Drigg and Irton; Rev. S. Pinhorne, Incumbent of Beckermont; Rev. Mr. Losh, Incumbent of Ponsonby; Rev. A. Walker, Vicar of Bootle; Rev. J. A. Cheese, Rector of Gosforth; Rev. Mr. Byrnas, Curate of Drigg and Irton; Rev. Mr. Wilkinson, Curate of Eskdale; Rev. W. Robinson, Incumbent of Muncaster; Rev. Mr. Watson, Curate of Waberthwaite; Rev. Mr. Manclark, Incumbent of Woodland. There were also present G. G. Mounsey, Esq., of Carlisle, the Bishop's Registrar; Messrs. Harper and Parke, the Churchwardens of Millom Church; Jos. S. Miers (sic.), Esq., Poorhouse; Mr. Sykes, Salthouse; Mrs. Pinhorne, Beckermont; Mrs. Robinson, Muncaster; Mr. and Mrs. Postlethwaite, Low House; Miss Jackson, Redhill, Millom; and the greater part of the respectable parishioners of Millom. A collection was made after the service, amounting to nearly £18.

Cumberland Pacquet and Ware's Whitehaven Advertiser – November 11th 1862

1865

HOUSE AT MILLOM SCHOOL

TENDERS

Persons desirous to tender for the erection of a small house at Millom School are requested to send in tenders to the Vicar.

Plans and specifications may be seen at Millom School on and after Monday, June 12th.

The Building Committee do not bind themselves to accept the lowest or any tender.

The Whitehaven News – Thursday, June 8th 1865

PRESENTATION OF AN ADDRESS TO THE REV. E. E. ALLEN, M.A

The following address has been lately presented by the clergy of the Rural Deanery of Gosforth, to the Rev. E. E. Allen, M.A., Vicar of Millom, and Rural Dean, who is about to leave this part of the country, having accepted the living of Porthkerry, in South Wales. Mr. Allen carries with him the sincere regard of all his numerous friends in this diocese, having obtained their esteem and affection by his courteous and Christian demeanour:-

TO THE REV. EDMUND EDWARD ALLEN, M.A., VICAR OF MILLOM AND RURAL DEAN.

"Dear Sir, The clergy of the rural deanery of Gosforth take this mode of bidding you farewell.

It is with mingled feelings of pleasure and sorrow that we subscribe our names to this parting salutation, sorrow that you will be removed from that intimate communion which has been maintained between us for the last eleven years, and pleasure at the thought that your energies will be transferred to a sphere where they will at least better remunerated, if not thoroughly valued.

Individually and collectively, we beg to assure you of our appreciation of the manner in which you have performed the duties of your office as our rural dean.

The quarterly meetings which have been held under your auspices have tended to draw closer the ties of common duties, by mutual intercourse in our somewhat straggling district, besides the benefits which we feel we have derived from the amicable discussion of subjects of common interest; and we thank you for the opportunities thus afforded us of obtaining a better acquaintance with yourself and with one another; trusting that you will carry away with you a not unpleasant recollection of the harmony which has prevailed under your kindly presidency.

When you recently conveyed our parting good wishes to our late venerable archdeacon, we had to lament that failing strength was the cause of the severance of the connexion between us; no such cause for regret diminishes the satisfaction with which we wish you 'God speed' in your new work, as you leave us with unabated strength, and in the vigour of a matured intellect to labour in another portion of the Lord's vineyard. Along with our prayers that His blessing may accompany you in your work, we venture to add to our confident belief that we shall hear a good report of your usefulness as a minister of Christ, as long as He shall enable you to preach His gospel; and our trust that distance will not entirely break off that intercourse to which we can look back only with pleasure.

We request your acceptance of the accompanying token of our brotherly kindness and esteem, and trust that it may assist in occasionally recalling to your memory, as years advance, the good wishes of your northern friends."

The Whitehaven News – Thursday, August 17th 1865

ECCLESIASTICAL INTELLIGENCE

The Duchy of Lancaster has presented the Rev. John Irving, M.A., of Worcester College, Oxford, Incumbent of Stainmore, near Brough, Westmorland, to the Vicarage of Millom, Cumberland, rendered vacant by the preferment of the Rev. Edmund Edward Allen.

Bell's Weekly Messenger – Saturday, November 4th 1865

1866

REV. E. E. ALLEN AND MILLOM SCHOOL

The late vicar of Millom, the Rev. E. E. Allen, during his incumbency made a vigorous effort to supply a long-felt want. Strange as it may seem, there was not till then a central school in the parish. Through Mr. Allen's exertions, ably backed by his parishioners, a school house, sufficiently commodious, was erected, and is now free from debt. A residence for the master was also commenced by him, and has been completed by his successor, the Rev. J. Irving. There is however, yet a debt of about £80 on the house. One recent donation of £10, and two donations of £5 each, by gentlemen connected with the works now going on near Holborn Hill, have reduced the debt to its present amount; and it is in contemplation to endeavour to reduce that amount by a series of these entertainments or readings now so general. It is proposed to hold the first of these on an early day, but whether they will be continued this spring, or be postponed till autumn, has not been definitely settled.

Ulverston Mirror and Furness Reflector – March 31st 1866

1870

REV. JOHN IRVING AND MISS JANE CHAMLEY MARRIAGE

MARRIAGES.

IRVING—CHAMLEY.—25th, at All Saints, Knightsbridge, by the Rev. John Percival, M.A., principal of Clifton College, Bristol, the Rev. John Irving, vicar of Millom, Cumberland, and rural dean of Gosforth, to Jane, second daughter of the late Matthew Chamley, Esq., of Warcop House, Westmorland.

London Evening Standard – Friday, May 27th 1870

MARRIAGE FESTIVITIES AT MILLOM

On Wednesday last there was a great display of bunting and other signs of rejoicings to celebrate the marriage of the much esteemed vicar, the Rev. John Irving, who was on that day married at All Saints, London. Amongst other mutual friends present were George Moore Esq., of Whitehall, and his lady. After the ceremony, the happy couple left for Folkstone *en route* to Switzerland. The shipping at Duddon harbour were decked in gay flags from mast head to deck, flags were also displayed at Millom Ironworks, the Hodbarrow Mines and by the tradesmen and others in Holborn Hill. Mr. Dobson erected a flag staff and a wide spread of bunting on the summit of Middle Brow, near the Hill in Millom. It must be gratifying to all interested to observe the warmth of feeling and kind regard evinced in the vicar's welfare

Ulverston Mirror and Furness Reflector – June 4th 1870

PRESENTATION

On Tuesday last, one of those pleasing events tending to cement and extend the kindly feeling which generally exists in rural districts between pastor and flock, took place at Millom Vicarage. The incumbent, the Rev. J. Irving, has lately brought to the parsonage a bride, and his parishioners, anxious to show the esteem which his efforts in their spiritual behalf has earned for him, each and all contributed their names to an address, which has been engrossed, and signed by 237 parishioners in the parish of Millom, and on Tuesday it, together with a handsome clock and candelabra, was presented to the rev. gentleman by Mr. Massicks. The address, engrossed upon vellum, was as follows:-

To the Reverend John Irving, Vicar of Millom, and Rural Dean.

"Reverend and Dear Sir – We, whose names are hereunto subscribed, being members of your congregation, gladly avail ourselves of the occasion of your marriage to congratulate you upon that happy event, and to assure you of the high esteem and affection with which we regard you. During the five years it has been our privilege to benefit by you ministrations in our venerable parish church, you have become endeared to us; and now that your parish is growing in population and importance, we trust the all-ruling Providence may grant you increased health and strength to administer the teachings of our beloved Church. In this high calling we doubt not you will be largely aided by the lady who will now, as your wife, share our regard and kindest wishes: and we desire to welcome her to Millom, and to hope that her residence amongst us may ever be agreeable. We are convinced that this address, having the names of so large a section of your congregation attached, will be more valued by you than any other evidence we could give of our good feeling; but we beg, in addition, that you will accept this clock and candelabra; and as time rolls on, may the hours it chimes be to you and to Mrs. Irving those of peace and happiness."

Mr. Irving made a most feeling reply, expressive of the universal kindness he had met with from the parishioners of every grade in the parish, and, he said, he could wish for no greater happiness than to spend the remainder of his life amongst them.

Soulby's Ulverston Advertiser and General Intelligencer – Thursday, July 7th 1870

1871

OLD VICARAGE

Millom Vicarage House for Sale.

TO BE SOLD BY AUCTION,
At the house of Henry Hodgson, White Horse Inn, The Hill, Millom, on Friday, July 28th, at 6 o'clock p.m.,

THE VICARAGE HOUSE and Premises, containing a good garden, barn, stable, and other conveniences.

751   JOHN COWARD, Auctioneer.

Soulby's Ulverston Advertiser and General Intelligencer – July 20th 1871

CORRESPONDENCE
MILLOM CHURCHYARD
To the Editor of the Ulverston Advertiser

Sir. – Much has been said about Kirkby Churchyard and the sheep, but I think that if we had only a few sheep in Millom Churchyard they would make an improvement. The ground is covered with rank grass and nettles above knee-deep, so that friends can scarcely point out the place where there departed relatives are laid. The vicar and curate have been very active in seeing that the services of the Church are better conducted than they once were; and I think that, that worthy functionary the clerk, might copy their laudable example, and improve the appearance of the Churchyard. I feel sure there are plenty of people in Millom, who would willingly mow it for the sake of the grass. The Advertiser has done much good in Millom, by giving publicity to many abuses, and I hope that we shall shortly see a better state of things in Millom Churchyard. Yours truly, DECENCY. Holborn Hill, July 16th, 1871.

Soulby's Ulverston Advertiser and General Intelligencer – July 20th 1871

NEW VICARAGE

To Builders and Contractors.

TENDERS will be received for the Erection of a NEW VICARAGE HOUSE and Outbuildings, at Millom, by Messrs. Paley and Austin, Lancaster, or by the Rev. I. Irving, Millom Vicarage, up to August 28th.

Plans and Specifications may be seen at Millom Vicarage from Aug. 14 to Aug. 21, and at the office of Messrs. Paley and Austin, Lancaster, from Aug. 21st to Aug. 28th.

Soulby's Ulverston Advertiser and General Intelligencer – August 10th 1871

A FEMALE SEXTON

On Saturday last, there died at Holborn Hill, Millom, Mrs. Betty Crellin, in her 75th year, a woman generally esteemed throughout the district. Her father was parish clerk of Millom (Page 1), and when age and infirmities necessitated the use of two sticks to the old man, his daughter filled his place in all labour departments of the office, and for some years she regularly dug graves, tolled the bell, &c. Her memory, too, was remarkably good, and she had a thorough knowledge of and could point out to the relatives the exact place in the churchyard which marked the resting-place of the departed. Her remains were interred on the 28th inst.

Penrith Observer – December 5th 1871

1872

LAYING OF THE FOUNDATION STONE FOR NEW VICARAGE

Holy Trinity Vicarage 2023, now a private residence. Image © Bry Cooper. Permission to reproduce here granted by Mr. A. Slack

An interesting event took place at Millom on Monday last, viz., the laying of the foundation stone of a New Vicarage House. The old Vicarage House stood near the Church, and was destroyed in the time of the rebellion, about 200 years ago. After that time the Incumbents of the parish had to dwell in tents until a small house, a mile and a half distant from the Parish Church, was purchased for the living about the year 1790, and this since that time has been the residence of the Incumbents of the parish. A new house was very much needed, and the present Incumbent has been the means of providing funds for this object. The foundation stone was laid by Mrs. Irving, in the presence of a few friends, and a short religious service was performed on the occasion. Mr. Paley, of Lancaster, is the architect, and Mr. Hodgson, Holborn Hill, is the builder. The workmen, to the number of 12, were entertained at a supper in the evening.

Lancaster Gazette – January 20th 1872

1887

PRESENTATION TO THE REV. T. HACKWORTH

On Tuesday evening the pleasing ceremony of presenting a testimonial to the Rev. T. Hackworth, curate of Holy Trinity Parish, Millom, took place in the Mission Room, Holborn Hill, after the usual weekly evening service. The room was nicely filled. The presentation took the form of a cheque, which had been subscribed to by the parishioners and admirers generally. The Rev. J. Irving, vicar of Holy Trinity, in making the presentation, spoke in high terms of Mr. Hackworth's good qualities and of the high regard in which he is held in Millom. So much did Mr. Irving feel Mr. Hackworth's leaving that he actually broke down. Mr. Hackworth replied in a very feeling speech, and said he was very sorry to leave him; but, as it was the wish of the Bishop, he could not do otherwise. He thanked them most cordially for their kindness. A handsome inkstand is also to be presented to him, as well as other presents. Mr. Hackworth leaves Millom on Friday for Workington, where he takes the senior curacy of St. Michael's Parish. We understand that the Rev. Mr. Atkinson, of Newcastle, is to take Mr. Hackworth's place.

Soulby's Ulverston Advertiser and General Intelligencer – August 25th 1887

1889

RESTORATION OF THE OLD CHURCH

On Friday evening last a meeting was held by the parishioners to consider the means to be adopted to restore the Holy Trinity Church. Certain alterations are to be effected, including cleaning the interior and the erection of a belfry and turret. The expenses incurred are expected to amount to £200. It was resolved at the meeting that the rent of the school-house should be devoted to the restoration fund. It is to be regretted that some steps have not been taken to remove certain so-called improvements, which, some years ago, were made, and to restore the venerable building to its original appearance. Such a scheme would meet with the hearty approval of the Vicar.

Cumberland Pacquet and Ware's Whitehaven Advertiser – July 25th 1889

AN AMUSING INCIDENT

It appears that a goat, belonging to the Castle Farm, made its way into the Parish Church on Sunday Evening, through a door which had been left open to cool the sanctuary. Presumably it had gained admittance unknown to the faithful warder of the door, who promptly ejected the intruder. Nanny, however, not to be outdone by his discourteous treatment, quietly marched around the outside of the church and put in an appearance at the chancel door.

Barrow Herald and Furness Advertiser – August 10th 1889

GAS AND WATER COMMITTEE

An application was made by the vicar and churchwardens of Millom Old Church that the Board should lay gas pipes from Holborn Hill to the boundary of their district, for the purpose of supplying gas to the church and of lighting the footpath thereto across the fields when required. The committee having referred to the correspondence and minutes in the matter of five years ago, recommended that the offer then made by the Board be renewed, and the pipes laid subject to a grant of easement being obtained from Lord Lonsdale's trustees, and to the church authorities guaranteeing that gas shall be used in the church. The Clerk was instructed to make application for the easement, and the surveyor was authorised to ascertain the number of lamps required for the footpath.

Cumberland Pacquet and Ware's Whitehaven Advertiser – October 10th 1889

THE PROPOSED GAS SUPPLY TO THE MILLOM OLD CHURCH

The supply of gas to the Millom Old Church was under the consideration of the Millom Local Board on Tuesday. The following letters respecting the easement for the pipes and erections of lamps were read by the Clerk:-

Whitehaven, October 29th 1889.

Dear Sir, - Gas Pipes Easement to Millom Church and Privilege of Erecting Gas Lamps. I have your letter of the 23rd. ult., asking for permission to allow the Millom Local Board to lay gas pipes through Lord Lonsdale's land to Millom Church, and to erect five gas lamps as shown on tracing accompanying letter, and in reply, beg to say that I am willing to allow the pipes to be laid, and the gas lamps to be erected on the following terms and conditions:- 1. The Millom Local Board to pay Lord Lonsdale the sum of 5s. per annum for the gas pipe easement from Martinmas, 11th November next, and 2s 6d. per annum, from the same date, for the whole fie gas lamps. 2. The Board to compensate the tenants of the land for any damage caused by laying the pipes. 3. The pipes must not be nearer the surface of the land than two feet. 4. The easement for pipes and privilege of having the gas lamps, will be subject to removal on six months notice from any date. With regard to your application on behalf of the Vicar and Churchwardens, I am willing that the gas pipes should be laid, and the one gas lamp erected as shown in the tracing on the above condition, except with regard to payment. In this case I propose to charge 2s. 6d. per annum for the pipes, and 6d. per annum for the gas lamps. The whole of the work to be done on Lord Lonsdale's agent's satisfaction. I shall be glad to hear that this is agreed to. Yours faithfully, R. A. ROBINSON. W. T. Lawrence, Esq., Solicitor, Millom.

Ulverston, October 30th 1889.

Dear Sir, In reply to yours of the 23rd ult., as to lamps being erected along the footpath leading to the Parish Church, at Millom, on behalf of Mrs. Finch, we have great pleasure in consenting to the proposal, and the Board can proceed. Of course, the Board would arrange and pay the tenants in case of damage being done to them in carrying out the work, but we infer there will not be any damage done as the Board will keep to the footpath. Yours, &c., SETTLE & FARMER. W. T. Lawrence, Esq., Local Board, Millom.

Mr. Vaughan remarked that according to the terms contained in Lord Lonsdale's letter, the church might at any time be kept in darkness by giving six months notice. It would be better to make arrangements in perpetuity. It would not be advisable to go to the expense of laying pipes, &c., under such terms. The Clerk stated that it would entail an outlay of £150 to carry the work to the Board's boundary, and £30 to have the remainder of the work done. Mrs. Finch did not charge anything for the easement. Mr. Vaughan thought when the terms of Mrs. Finch were made known he would also grant the easement on the same conditions. Mr. Johnson proposed that the Clerk write to Lord Lonsdale's agent, and endeavour to get the easement in perpetuity. In seconding the proposition, Mr. Nicholson said he could not see that it would be right to go to such expense on an arrangement that could be terminated any time. The subject therefore stood over for a further communication from Lord Lonsdale's agent.

Cumberland Pacquet and Ware's Whitehaven Advertiser – November 7th 1889

1892

NEW MEMORIAL WINDOW FOR MILLOM CHURCH

**Thomas Whinnerah memorial window in the East wall of the Chancel at Holy Trinity Church.
Image © Bry Cooper**

Thomas Whinnerah memorial window inscription. Image © Bry Cooper

"IN MEMORY OF THOMAS WHINNERAH OF NORTH ADELAIDE SOUTH AUSTRALIA MERCHANT BORN AT DUNNINGWELL IN THIS PARISH ON THE 19TH APRIL 1809 DIED IN ADELAIDE SOUTH AUSTRALIA ON THE 18TH JULY 1890"

At the Carlisle Consistory Court, yesterday (Wednesday), Chancellor Ferguson heard a case in which the Rev. John Irving, M.A., vicar of Holy Trinity, Millom, and the churchwardens, Mr. William Lucas Benn, Mr. Henry Frankland Fox and Mr. James Wilson Brockbank, applied for a faculty to enable them to take out the old glass in the east window of the chancel of the church, and to insert in lieu thereof stained glass in memory of the late Mr. Thomas Whinnerah, of Adelaide, South Australia, who was a native of the district.

The Registrar (Mr. Bowman) intimated that Mr. Irving was laid up with influenza, and had asked him to make the application on his behalf. Mr. Irving had written to say that there was no objection on the part of the parishioners.

A sketch of this window was submitted. The subject is "The Last Supper," and the artists are Messrs. Clayton and Bell. The window is being put in at the expense of Miss Whinnerah, of Broughton-in-Furness, as sister of the late Mr. Whinnerah.

The Chancellor ordered the faculty should issue.

Soulby's Ulverston Advertiser and General Intelligencer - January 21st 1892

HOLY TRINITY

HARVEST THANKSGIVING SERVICE

The Holy Trinity harvest thanksgiving services were held on Sunday in the Parish Church. The Parish Church was suitably decorated by Mrs. Irving and the Misses Irving, Miss Meakin, Miss Stoney, Mrs. Lewthwaite and other lady members of the Girl's Bible Class. The altar was adorned with a large and beautifully constructed floral cross, and the vases filled with choice white lilies. The pulpit and lectern were decorated with wreaths of wheat, corn and gladioli interspersed with clusters of grapes. The font was surmounted by a cross of white dahlias, China asters standing out from a mass of ferns, corns and blackberry sprays. On the north side of the nave were the words " The Reapers are the Angels," beautifully worked in white flannel and ornamented with ears of corn and flowers. The vicar preached in the morning, and delivered an excellent discourse to a large congregation. The assistant curate (the Rev. W. P. Ingledow) gave the address in the evening, the church being crowded, necessitating, as usual, the use of chairs in the aisles. Mr. John Hall officiated at the organ, special psalms, hymns, anthems &c., being sung. Supplies of corn &c., were kindly sent by Mr. G. Postlethwaite, Mr. John Watson and others. The offerings realised about £4.

The Millom Gazette – Saturday, October 1st 1892

1893

BAZAAR AT MILLOM

Last Wednesday afternoon a bazaar was opened by Mrs. Myers (Dunningwell), in the County Hall, Millom, in connection with Holy Trinity Church, with the object of raising funds for the repairs of heating apparatus at Millom Parish Church; for adding a room to The Hill Chapel, and for repairs of The Hill Chapel and Parish room, Holborn Hill. The stalls, six in number, were laden with a large and varied assortment of useful and ornamental articles. The Rev. J. Irving, vicar of Holy Trinity Church, in calling upon Mrs. Myers to declare the bazaar open, expressed the thanks and gratitude of all present to Mrs. Myers and those ladies who had so kindly taken stalls at that bazaar. Mrs. Myers briefly declared the bazaar open, and hoped that by the next evening nothing would be left on the stall but the decorations. The bazaar was continued yesterday (Thursday).

Maryport Advertiser – Saturday, August 5th 1893

1895

PAINFUL SCENE IN A MILLOM CHURCH

SUDDEN ILLNESS OF THE VICAR OF HOLY TRINITY

On Sunday morning last, during the progress of the ordinary morning service at Holy Trinity Church, Millom, the vicar, the Rev. J. Irving, who occupied the pulpit, became suddenly indisposed. The former part of the service had proceeded as usual, but after announcing the well-known hymn, "All people that on earth do dwell," previous to taking the ante-Communion Service, the aged vicar was seen to suddenly stagger and fall down in a faint in the pulpit. Fortunately, Miss Irving, his daughter, perceived his condition, and caught him as he fell. After a lapse of a few minutes the rev. gentleman seemed to revive, and persisted in proceeding with the service. However, after labouring under difficulties for a while, he again broke down, and was removed to the vestry. Medical aid was at once summoned, and the rev. gentleman was removed to his home. The service was thus brought to an abrupt termination, and the assembled parishioners, who were much upset at the painful incident, quietly dispersed. In the afternoon of the same day, the rev. gentleman persisted in travelling to Kirksanton to conduct the service, walking both ways, a matter for congratulation.

The Millom Gazette – November 16th 1895

1896

BURIAL GROUND CONSECRATION AT MILLOM

On Wednesday the Bishop of the Diocese consecrated a piece of ground which has been added to the burial ground attached to Holy Trinity Church, Millom. The clergy present were Archdeacon Phillips, Revs. J. Irving, A. E. Joscelyne, J. Haslam, T. Metcalfe, W. P. Ingledow, W. Kewley, W. Sykes, &c. Before proceeding to the ground the Bishop gave an impressive address from the 14th chapter of the Book of Revelation, 13th verse, "Blessed are the dead which die in the Lord," &c, in the course of which he observed that the graveyard about to be consecrated was a sleeping place. As they knew the name frequently given to these graveyards under certain conditions was "cemeteries" and a cemetery meant a sleeping place. Let them try not only for their own sakes but for the sakes of their children to look on death in the right light, let them try and think of death as being something which must be very sad in the separation which is brought about for a time, but nevertheless as being full of comfort that they lived with Christ and died in Christ then even death came with a benediction. He trusted that henceforth they would not only think of their dear old Church as the House of God but they would also think of the neighbouring Churchyard which surrounded it as a place where they would, when their time came, be laid to sleep, and that those who stood over their graves would be comforted with the words " Blessed are the dead which die in the Lord"; yea even so saith the Spirit for they rest from their labours and their works do follow them."

The Millom Gazette – Saturday, August 15th 1896

MILLOM OLD CHURCH

The other day the ceremony of laying the foundation stone of a new Parish Hall for St. George's district was performed. To any one at all inclined to antiquarian researches such a scene was witnessed at the stone-laying must bring to mind something of the condition of things when the foundation stone of the first place of worship in this district was laid. Millom Old Church has weathered the storms of so many centuries that little appears to have been known of its first use as a place of worship. It was rectorial till the year 1228 when it was given to the Abbey of St. Mary in Furness. The building would evidently have been in existence long before this. It is quite probable that Saxon Christians came to worship in a building on or near the site of the present Church. As the main road led past the Castle from over the sands, this would probably be looked on as comparatively a more public place in days prior to the Norman Conquest than what it is at the present day. The peculiar window known as the "Fish Window" near the organ bears evidence of its existence in the early days of Christianity. It is true that there are local traditions associating this window in some way with the superiority of Haverigg flukes, but the more reasonable explanation for the existence of this window is the tradition that the early Christians, in fear of their Pagan persecutors, utilised this emblem as an indication of their religion. If this tradition is anything like authenticated then Millom Old Church must be classed amongst the most ancient Christian establishments in the country. The fact that it is nearly 700 years since the living was deemed worthy of being attached to Furness Abbey indicates that there must have been a place of worship here long prior to that date. Not only was the living capable of maintaining the officiating clergyman but we find that one moiety was reserved by Walter de Grey, Archbishop of York, to be assigned in 1230 for the maintenance of three chaplains with clerks and other charges for the support of his chantry of St. Nicholas in the metropolitan Church of York. The Old Church will no doubt have undergone many vicissitudes during its history. It will have had to withstand the assaults of the Scotch raiders more than once. Could the old walls speak, what a strange history they might unfold! Here, for generation after generation, the remains of those who have spent their lives in the district have been deposited. As the old burial ground was found inadequate to supply all the space needed for hundreds of years as a last resting place for the remains of many generations of Millomites, within recent years the cemetery has had to be enlarged and this year a further portion of ground had to be set apart for sepulchral purposes. The glory of the old Lords of Millom has departed from the place, but an ancient mural tablet still bears evidence of the position which the Hudleston family once maintained. There is close to this tablet an altar tomb with Gothic tracery, &c., on which recline the effigies of a knight and his lady; both are, however, in a very mutilated condition and were no doubt at one time intended to commemorate some more than usual prominent ancestor of the Hudleston family, probably the Sir John Hudleston who espoused Joan, sister of Sir John Seymour, an aunt of Jane Seymour, Queen consort of Henry VIII. The churchyard contains the remains of a cross, the shaft of which is charged with four shields. Many alterations have been effected from time to time; most of the old windows have been replaced by those of more modern design. A few years ago gas was laid to the church which until then was lighted by oil lamps. Near the eastern window the ancient piscina was located, and at the west end there is the octagon stone font, ornamented with quatrefoils and a shield charged with the arms of the Hudlestons. The living was valued in the King's Book at £8 5s. 8d. and was certified to the Governors of Queen Anne's bounty as of the annual value of £26 1s. 8d. About the year 1721 it was augmented with £256 left by the Rev. John Postlethwaite, master of St. Paul's School, London, and about the same time with £200 form the Governors of Queen Anne's Bounty. Both these sums appear to have been expended in the purchase of an estate called Fawcett Bank, near Sedbergh, in Yorkshire. The old vicarage was of a very rough construction, but the splendid modern building located near Gilscaur, on the confines of Millom Park, is replete with every requirement. The Parish Register commences in 1598. Amongst the Vicars known to have held the living are Edmund Staneforth, 1535; Roger Askew, 1661; William Wels, 1670; Joseph Taylor, 1699; Thomas Benn, 1713; Matthew Postlethwaite, 1743; Edward Nicholson, 1778; John Smith, 1781; John Bolton, 1797; John Smith, 1821; Henry Dixon, 1822; Henry Pickthall, 1836; Edmund Allen B.A., 1855.

The Millom Gazette – Saturday, October 17th 1896

1898

STONEY FAMILY TRAGEDIES

The grave of Jessie Mary Stoney, eldest daughter of former Physician and Coroner of Millom, Dr. Pery Butler Stoney, in Holy Trinity Churchyard. Also commemorated on the headstone is her brother, Elkin Percy Stoney, whose death was announced on the day his sister was interred. Sadly, no remnants of the grave are visible today.

SAD DEATH OF A DOCTOR'S DAUGHTER

Quite a painful impression was made on the inhabitants of Millom on Sunday night when it became known that Miss Mamie Stoney, aged about 25 years (eldest daughter of Dr. P. B. Stoney, coroner for the liberty of Millom and the oldest physician in the town), had died under circumstances which have caused the family and those who had the pleasure of the acquaintance of the young lady the most profound grief. Only on the Tuesday previous Miss Stoney, who has always shown great willingness to assist in parochial work, whether in connection with St. George's or Holy Trinity parishes, attended the annual service in the last-named parish and contracted a chill. She was, however, out cycling on Thursday, but on Saturday found it necessary to remain indoors. Nothing serious was apprehended, and her mother left for Scotland on Saturday. On Sunday evening she was in her room with her sister, Miss Fanny, whom she was recommending to go to church instead of staying with her. Her sister left the room for a moment, but immediately was startled by the sudden ringing of Miss Stoney's bedroom bell, and on hurrying back, found, to her horror, that she was black in the face and fast choking. The assistance of neighbours was called, but in less than five minutes the young lady was beyond earthly help, the cause of death being an acute attack of quinsy. Only on Saturday morning Dr. Stoney returned home eldest son on board ship enroute for India. Dr. Stoney, who is prostrated with the heavy blow which has befallen the family, unfortunately could not be got on the scene quickly enough to render any assistance, Mrs. Stoney only arrived home on Monday night, and her grief on finding for the first time of their terrible loss can be better imagined than described, the deceased being much beloved by all who knew her.

Maryport Advertiser – February 26th 1898

DEATH OF MR. ELKIN STONEY

Our readers will have heard with the deepest regret of the death at sea of Mr. Elkin Stoney, eldest son of Dr. Stoney, whilst he was on his passage to India. The deepest sympathy is felt with Dr. and Mrs. Stoney in their sad bereavement, as it was only the previous week that the death occurred of their eldest daughter. Mr. Elkin Stoney was 18 years of age, and for some time has been a student in St. Bartholomew's Hospital, London. He left that institution a few weeks ago and was on his way to India to take up a post he had secured there. At the time of starting he was far from well, and a telegram was received by Dr. Stoney this week, announcing his death on the same day that the remains of his sister were interred at Holy Trinity Church.

The Millom Gazette – March 4th 1898

DEATH OF CANON ALLEN
THIRTY YEARS RECTOR OF PORTHKERRY

We regret to announce the death of the Rev. Canon Allen, rector of Porthkerry, which took place at Porthkerry Vicarage at 4 o'clock on Sunday morning. Deceased was 76 years of age, had been in failing health for some time, and was attended by Dr. Neale, but his demise was somewhat unexpected. His familiar figure will be greatly missed in the Barry district, where he was actively identified himself with all kinds of religious work, being looked up and respected alike by both Churchmen and Non-Conformists, with the latter of whom he has often been found in co-operation. Owing to his active religious spirit he earned for himself the title locally of "Bishop of Barry." He was a member of the Barry Nursing Association, of which his daughter is hon. Secretary. He was also a member of the local Vigilance Association. The deceased was appointed to the prebendal stall of Taviwell, Llandaff Cathedral in 1887, but never preached in the Cathedral.

The illness that has resulted fatally was due to influenza, but the worst symptoms, it was thought, had passed away, and the aged patient was ordered to his room only as a precautionary measure. He passed away so peacefully in his sleep that his youngest daughter, who was watching at his bedside, did not notice that life had departed until the thought was impressed upon her by the solemn stillness which pervaded the room.

Edmund Edward Allen, M.A., of Trinity College, Cambridge, rector of Porthkerry and Barry, hon. Canon of Llandaff, rural dean of Llandaff Lower Western Division, was the second son of Lancelot Baugh Allen, of Cilrhiw, Pembrokeshire, by his wife, the daughter of Thomas Peter Romilly, brother to the great Sir Samuel Romilly. He was born when George the Fourth was King. He was educated at Westminster School, King's College, London and Trinity College, Cambridge, and in 1847 he was ordained to the curacy of St. Mary's, Shrewsbury. After returning for a time to the curacy of Clarbeston, in his native county, in 1854, he was promoted to the living of Millom, in Cumberland, where he remained till 1865, and where he was also Rural Dean of Gosforth. In 1865 he was presented to the rectory of Porthkerry and Barry by his relatives, the then surviving sons of Sir S. Romilly. Here he lived for more than 30 years the peaceful, quiet life of a country parson. It was an ideal life, full of charm, especially to Mr. Allen. From this peaceful life, the rector and his flock were rudely shaken in 1884 by the starting of Barry Dock. The time had come to test what material the rector of Barry was made off and he did not fail to rise to the opportunity. A temporary church was erected for the district of St. Paul's, East Barry, and later the Barry Parish Hall and Sunday School were opened, the erection of which cost about £1,000. How much the rector's personality had to do with the successful undertaking of these works will be readily acknowledged by those who helped him. That the work of managing such a parish as Barry is now should not be so congenial to the rector's spirit was only natural. It was hard that, after 20 years of his vigorous manhood spent in the peaceful pastorate of a quiet flock, the shepherd should exchange, when the leaf is sear, his free calm mountain side for the turmoil of a town. In nothing did this rude awakening disturb the rector more than in his political beliefs. Hitherto, in spite of his surroundings, the rector had been true to the political faith of the Allens and the Romillys, of broad, earnest and advanced Liberalism. The sudden change in his life and circumstances, aided by the adoption of a plan of Home Rule by Mr. Gladstone, lost to the Liberal party a very sincere and valuable member.

Cardiff Times and South Wales Weekly News – Saturday, April 9th 1898

1899

LATE CANON ALLEN OF BARRY

UNVEILING OF MEMORIAL WINDOWS

The movement for honouring the memory of the late Canon Allen who for 33 years was rector of Barry and Porthkerry parishes, reached its consummation to-day, when the Lord Bishop of Llandaff attended at both places and conducted dedication services of memorial windows at the respective churches. Shortly after noon the Bishop, who was supported by a number of local clergy, performed the ceremony at Porthkerry, where the Rev. Z. Price, of St. Paul's Church, Barry, preached an appropriate sermon, in the course of which he referred to the noble character of the late beloved rector, who was held in high esteem by all religious denominations. The windows in that quaint church, situate on the eastern end of the building above the Communion table, are representations of St. Peter and St. John. Beneath the former are the words "Persecuted, but not forsaken," and below the figure of St. John, "A disciple whom Jesus loved." Then appears the inscription, "To the glory of God, and in memory of Edmund Edward Allen, hon. canon of Llandaff and rural dean, rector of the parish, 1865-98." The service was exceedingly simple but impressive throughout. In the afternoon, at Barry Parish Church, the Bishop of Llandaff preached.

South Wales Echo – Wednesday, November 22nd 1899

1900

THE DRILL HALL CHANGES HANDS

The large building now known as the Drill Hall in Holborn Hill, but which was formerly the Town Hall, has changed hands. On Tuesday, Mr. A. Coward put it up for auction. After some slow bidding it was knocked down to Mr. James Howarth for £435. The purchase was, however, made for Dr. Stoney and the Rev. W. S. Sykes for Holy Trinity parish. The building, it is understood, will be used as the Young Men's Bible Class. It is undoubtedly a great acquisition for Holy Trinity parish, and the purchasers have been fortunate in securing the building on such reasonable terms. Mr. W. T. Lawrence, solicitor, had the carriage of the sale.

The Millom Gazette – Friday, March 2nd 1900

EVENTS OF THE WEEK

The Rev. H. V. Banks, who preached his farewell sermons at St. Gabriel's Mission Church, Blackburn, on Sunday, has accepted a curacy at Millom Church, which is situated in the diocese of Carlisle. The rev. gentleman contemplates commencing his new duties early in September, and has now left on a holiday.

The Blackburn Weekly Standard and Express – Saturday, August 4th 1900

REV. W. S. SYKES ACCEPTS THE VICARAGE OF ESKDALE

The Rev. R. H. Snape, who has resigned the living of Eskdale and accepted that of St. Bees, will be succeeded by the Rev. W. S. Sykes, who has been offered the living of Eskdale, which he has accepted. He is to be followed in the curacy of Holy Trinity Church, Millom by the Rev. Mr. Baker of Kendal

The Millom Gazette – Friday, August 31st 1900

PRESENTATION TO REV. W. S. SYKES

A presentation was made to the Rev. W. S. Sykes at the Holborn Hill Mission Room on Wednesday evening on the occasion of his leaving the parish to take up work in the adjacent parish of Eskdale. Amongst those present were: Rev. T. H. Banks, Mrs. Stoney, Mrs. Hill, Miss Irving, Miss Stoney, Mr. H. F. Fox, Mr. Cartwright and others. The presentation was made by Mr. H. F. Fox, who referred to the good work which Mr. Sykes had done during his five years residence in the Holy Trinity Parish. The presents consisted of a silver kettle and silver match box suitably inscribed, and were subscribed for by the parishioners. The Rev. W. S. Sykes thanked the donors in feeling terms for their handsome presents.

The Millom Gazette – Friday, October 19th 1900

1901

TRAGIC DEATH OF A CLERGYMAN AT MILLOM
CURATE DROPS DOWN DEAD IN A WAITING ROOM

The grave of Henry Villiers-Banks in Holy Trinity Churchyard

"Erected by the parishioners of Holy Trinity, Millom in loving memory of the Rev. Henry Villiers-Banks who died 21 Jan 1901 aged 38 years. Blessed are the dead which die in the Lord"

Quite a painful sensation was caused in Millom on Monday morning when it became known that the Rev. Henry Villiers-Banks, curate of Holy Trinity Church, Millom, had died with appalling suddenness. From what we have been able to gather, it appears that Mr. Banks, who resided with Mrs. Jenkinson, at Flora Villa, Finch Street arose as usual about seven o'clock on Monday morning, and at that time appeared in his usual state of health. After partaking of breakfast he left the house at a quarter to eight with the intention of catching the 8 o'clock train. The deceased gentleman had not long been absent from the house when he returned, as though he had forgotten something. In a short time he again left the house and proceeded to the railway station. Here he entered into conversation with Dr. Stoney in the waiting room. Suddenly, without the slightest warning, the rev. gentleman fell to the floor, and expired almost immediately. Everything possible was done for the deceased, and life having been pronounced extinct, the body was conveyed to deceased's residence. The cause of death is supposed to be heart disease. The facts were reported to the coroner, who under the circumstances deemed an inquest unnecessary. The deceased rev. gentleman was only 36 years of age, and what lends additional sadness to his almost tragic end is the fact that he had only been at Millom some four months, having succeeded the Rev. W. S. Sykes in October last. In Millom, and particularly by the parishioners of Holy Trinity, the deceased gentleman will be missed, for although his sojourn here had been brief, he had by his many excellent qualities endeared himself to a wide circle of friends, who now mourn their loss.

THE FUNERAL

The funeral took place on Wednesday afternoon, at the Holy Trinity Church, Millom. It was intended at first to have the funeral on Thursday, but when the deceased's relatives arrived other arrangements were made. The funeral service was conducted by the Rev. J. Irving (vicar), assisted by the Revs. W. S. Sykes (vicar of Eskdale) and W. P. Ingledow (vicar of Whicham formerly curates at Holy Trinity Church), and the Rev. A. E. Wyatt (St. George's). The funeral was attended by a very large number of persons mostly parishioners of Holy Trinity, and the numbers would have been augmented, but for the general impression in the town that the funeral was to take place on the Thursday. The members of the Young Men's Bible Class provided the bearers, and the Sunday School teachers also accompanied the remains of the deceased on the last mournful journey. The chief mourners were the deceased's brother and the young lady to whom he was to be shortly married, and for whom the greatest sympathy was felt in her bereavement. There were also present: The Rev. W. Stratton, Mrs. And Misses Irving, Mr. and Mrs. Johnstone, Dr. Stoney, Mrs. Yarr, Mr. Dixon, Mr. Watson, Mrs. Fearon, Mr. Ormandy, Mr. Morgan, Mr. H. F. Fox, &c.

The Millom Gazette – Friday, January 25th 1901

MRS. IRVING DEATH AND FUNERAL

DEATHS.

IRVING.—On the 29th ult., at The Vicarage, Millom, Jane, wife of the Rev. John Irving, aged 68 years.

The Millom Gazette – Friday, August 2nd 1901

The funeral of the late Mrs. Irving, wife of the Rev. J. Irving, vicar of Holy Trinity Church, took place on Thursday last, amid widespread manifestations of regret and sympathy. Deceased was formerly a Miss Chamley, of Warcop, Westmorland, and since her marriage, thirty years ago, has resided in Millom. She always took a deep interest in her husband's parish work, and by her uniform kindness greatly endeared herself to the parishioners generally. The interment service was conducted by the Rev. Canon Bell, of Muncaster, and Rev. G. Yorke, curate of Holy Trinity; and the large assemblage of mourners included the relatives, vicarage servants, local clergy, and many personal friends and parishioners. A number of beautiful wreaths were placed on the grave. Mr. Birbeck, of Millom, was entrusted with the funeral arrangements.

Soulby's Ulverston Advertiser and General Intelligencer – August 8th 1901

PICKINGS FROM MILLOM CHURCHYARD
[FROM A CORRESPONDENT.]

Wild family headstone at Holy Trinity Church

It is not often one finds the records of deaths in one family, on tombstones, carried forward for over a century. Such applies to the Wilds, who were doubtless a family of good standing. Lawrance Wild appears to have been twice married, his first wife, Elizabeth, dying "Noby 17. 1714, aged 44 (probably November is meant) Lawrance died in 1719, aged 72; and his second wife, Bridget in 1739, aged 73. The next record is of William Wild, who died in 1762, aged 84; John Wyld, 1747, aged 42; and Frances Wild, 1766, aged 62. The adjoining stone continues the record to 1782, 1783, 1797 and up to 1827.

Miles Postlethwaite and family tomb in Holy Trinity Churchyard

On a copper plate, let in the memorial stone of Miles Postlethwaite, of Powhouse, who died in 1742, aged 73, is engraved the following:- "Also, Elizabeth, his only daughter, who died of smallpox, 16th October, 1758, aged 22 years." Then the following lines:-

> "Her soul informed with every softer grace,
> Youth's fairest honours opening in her face,
> Sweet as the Flow'r that drinks the vernal dew,
> As glossy bright, and ah, as transient too.
> Such was the maid, on whose untimely Herse,

Flows the sad tribute of this humble verse.
Attend ye Fair, ye Young, the moral lay:
The term of Youth, of Life, is but a day!"

Ephraim and Jane Fox headstone at Holy Trinity Church (no longer in this position)

The coincidence of husband and wife dying at the same age (by years) is noticeable on the tomb of "Ephraim Fox, who died February 1st, 1796, in his 86th year; also, Jane, his wife, who died November 28th, 1795, in her 86th year; after living together man and wife 62 years." The lines follow:-

"If we have been planted together in the likeness of His death,
We shall be also in the likeness of His resurrection."

Capt. John Newby and family headstone in Holy Trinity Churchyard

Another tomb bears the following record:- "Captain John Newby, of Haverigg, died February 4th 1814, aged 66 years."

> "My Glass is run, my Grave you see,
> Prepare in time to follow me.
> Go home, my friends, and shed no tears,
> I must lie here till Christ appears."

An abounding faith seems to have inspired the inscription of the following lines on another memorial:-

> "I am not lost but gone before To learn and labour all the more."
> "Out of affliction Thou O God didst deliver me."

John McGowan and family headstone in Holy Trinity Churchyard

On the stone erected to the memory of John McGowan, of Holborn Hill, aged 53, are the following lines:-

> "Short and precarious is this life of ours,
> Feeble as grass, and frail as blooming flowers.
> May God protect from adverse wind,
> The tender plant which I have left behind.
> A long farewell, dear wife, I bid to you,
> My brethren all, and social friends, adue."

Soulby's Ulverston Advertiser and General Intelligencer – Thursday, October 10th 1901

UNVEILING OF A MEMORIAL AT HOLY TRINITY CHURCH, MILLOM

George Mason Park memorial tablet. Image © Bry Cooper

One of these similar events, which are always shrouded under a shadow of gloom, took place at Holy Trinity Church, Millom, on Sunday afternoon last. A special service was held on the occasion of the unveiling of a tablet erected in the above church to perpetuate the memory of a young man, a native of this parish, who lost his life in the early stages of the war in South Africa. The service was fixed for three o'clock, but long before that hour the church was crowded, every space being occupied. The service commenced by the singing of the 228th hymn, "Jerusalem, the Golden," followed by evening prayer, with special psalms and lesson. The hymn, 447 "Soldiers who are Christ's below," was sung, Mr. John Hall, the organist, accompanying. Afterwards the Rev. G. Yorke, curate, who conducted the service, proceeded down the aisle to the place of dedication, accompanied by the churchwardens (Mr. T. J. Newby and Mr. H. F. Fox), together with Major C. J. Myers, Dunningwell. Major Myers performed the duty of unveiling the memorial, whilst the clergyman read the dedication service. Then the anthem, "Abide with me," was played by the organist, Mr Keigwin singing the solos. Afterwards the Rev. G. Yorke preached a very effective sermon from 2nd Timothy, chapter 4, v. 7, "I have fought the good fight, I have finished my course," and in the course of his exhortations, appealed to his hearers to build up their monuments as true soldiers of Christ, and stand firm on duty, and then when the end came, let it come sudden or otherwise, what a glorious thing it would be after a well spent life, and in the fear of God to inherit eternal glory. After the sermon, hymn 437, "For all the saints, who from their labours rest," was sung with much feeling. At the end of the service, and whilst the large congregation was dispersing, the organist played "God save the King." The tablet bears the following inscription:- "In memory of George Mason Park (Private), Royal Lancaster Regiment, the beloved husband of Margaret Park, who was killed in action fighting for his Queen and country, on Spion Kop, South Africa, January 24th, 1900, in his 27th year. This was erected by friends." The tablet is a very handsome one, and was provided by Mr. G. Hill, monumental mason, Millom.

The Millom Gazette – Friday, December 5th 1901

1902

TESTIMONIAL TO THE REV. J. IRVING

During the past week the parishioners of Holy Trinity, Millom, have presented the Rev. J. Irving with a surplice and robes in recognition of his services and work during the last 35 years. We quote the following letter inserted by the Vicar in the "Parish Magazine" – "My dear friends and parishioners, I wish through the medium of our magazine to thank you all most heartily for your very kind present of a surplice and robes, which was presented to me this Easter. I am most deeply touched and gratified by your kind thought of me, and feel, that if it pleases God to spare me, I shall find my greatest happiness in working amongst you all for a few years longer. – Your sincere friend, JOHN IRVING.

The Millom Gazette – Friday, April 11th 1902

PRESENTATION AT MILLOM

The Rev. J. Irving, vicar of Millom, has been the recipient of a very handsome testimonial from his parishioners as a token of their affection and esteem. The gift took the form of a solid silver inkstand with inscription, silver candlesticks, silver paper knife, silver pen-wiper, and pen and pencil. On Thursday, after the evening service, the Vicar thanked his friends for their kindness. In the course of his address he feelingly referred to the sympathy the parish had specially shown to him during the last year of sorrow, and to the love which he had for the parish and the church, and that when he came to Millom nearly 37 years ago, he then expressed his wish that it might be the sphere of his life's work. The testimonial is now on view in Mr. Cartwright's window, St. George's Terrace.

The Millom Gazette – Friday, May 16th 1902

1904

HOLY TRINITY, MILLOM

Quite a pathetic incident, which occasioned much concern, occurred during the morning service at Holy Trinity Church, Millom, on Sunday last. The aged Vicar, the Rev. J. Irving, was preaching his sermon when he observed that he would not be able to continue his discourse and the fell back in the pulpit. Mr. W. J. Yarr and his daughter went to his assistance and he was conveyed home in his carriage as quickly as possible. We are glad to learn that the indisposition was soon over and that by evening e was much better; in fact, on Tuesday he was able to get out of doors again. It appears that he had unduly hastened to church, to which is attributed his sudden attack. That the rev. gentleman is no worse will be a source of relief and gratification to the public of Millom, with whom he is held in high esteem and veneration.

The Millom Gazette – Friday, March 25th 1904

REV. G. YORKE

The Rev. G. Yorke, who has been curate of Holy Trinity, Millom since 1901, has been presented by the Dean and Chapter of Carlisle to the Rectory of Bewcastle, in succession to the Rev. E. Walker

Maryport Advertiser – Saturday, October 8th 1904

HOLY TRINITY CURACY

We understand that the Rev. Mr. Davis, of Dublin has accepted the curacy of Holy Trinity in succession to the Rev. G. Yorke, who has been appointed to a living in the neighbourhood of Carlisle. On Sunday last the retiring curate preached his farewell sermon to a large congregation. Both Mr. and Mrs. Yorke have made many friends in Millom who wish them every success in their new parish.

The Millom Gazette – Friday, November 18th 1904

1905

Millom Parish Church Choir outside Holy Trinity Vicarage. Rev. John Irving seated middle of front row. Photo dated September 23rd 1905. Image © Millom Heritage & Arts Centre

1906

MILLOM POLICE COURT

The Millom magistrates had to listen to another sad case of juvenile crime, when on Saturday two schoolboys named Robert Dawson and John Moore, aged 11 and 10 respectively, appeared in charge of their parents, to answer an indictment of malicious and wilful damage to the tombstone of the late wife of the Rev. Canon Irving of Holy Trinity Church, Millom, on Sunday, the 10th June.

Mr. J. R. Hall, Millom, said he appeared on behalf of the informant, Capt. Thomas Chamley, who was a trustee, the will of the late Mrs. Irving. It was a case of wilful damage to property. The facts of the case were that the boys appeared on Sunday the 10th June to have gained access to the churchyard, and to cut out eight of the eleven letters which formed part of the inscription on the tombstone of the late Mrs. Irving. The boys were quite young, and were schoolboys. He believed there had been no previous offence against them and he was sure the Bench would feel it was a painful case and he did not want to press the convicton, although it was difficult to stop them. At the same time, there was a reign of terror at the churchyard, and the informant was obliged to appeal to the magistrates to stop the practice. It could not be allowed to continue.

In answer to the Clerk, the parents of the boys said they were not aware of their children's mischief.

Sergt. Armstrong said that on Tuesday the 12th June, he went to the Holy Trinity church yard and examined the tombstone, the property of Rev. Canon Irving, and found that eight letters had been removed, apparently by a knife or some other sharp instrument. The following day he went to the Holborn Hill School, where he saw the boys. He formally charged them. In reply, Moore said: "I only took about six out, and gave some of them to Dawson.

Dawson said in reply: "I was there, and it was Moore who cut them out and gave some to me."

Isaac Hill, son of George Hill, monumental mason, said he had seen the damage that had been done. There were eight letters and two spaces taken out, and the whole of the damage amounted to about 5s.

Mr. Moore, father of one of the boys, said they were punished for the offence by the Sunday School Superintendent and Miss Irving, who gave them to understand that nothing more would be heard about it. The Sunday School Superintendent went to his house, and said that if the boys were kept away from the Sunday School treat he thought it would be sufficient punishment for them.

The Clerk: Mr. and Miss Irving have not said anything, have they?

Mr. Moore: The Superintendent came to our house and told us. Miss Irving came, instructed by the superintendent.

The Chairman: They were kept away from the Sunday School treat as a punishment.

Mr. Hall: This is not exactly a case of boys taking a rabbit, or stealing apples, I don't press for a conviction.

The Chairman: You thought of doing it indirectly, after all.

After a brief consultation with his two colleagues, Mr. Walker said the Bench wished to be very lenient, but at the same time they thought it would be much better if they (the parents) were to punish the boys themselves. It was really a disgrace to go back and break into a public place like that. They would be let off if the parents would pay the expenses of the court, pay for the damage, and promise to punish the boys.

The cost of the court would be 8s. each, and the damage 5s., which was 2s. 6d. each, making a fine of 10s. 6d. each.

The Millom Gazette – Friday, July 27th 1906

CHURCH INSTITUTE AT MILLOM

For some time, those connected with Holy Trinity Church, Millom, have felt the want of an institute where they could meet together for social and other purposes. It has been decided to erect such a building at the corner of Cambridge Street and Holborn Hill. It will be made of bricks and be two storeys high. On the ground floor there will be a billiard room, smoking and reading room etc. Upstairs there will be a large room capable of accommodating 200 people, which can be used for parish purposes. The Institute will prove of great value to the parish of the old church. Subscriptions have been invited, and there is being a generous response, and preparations are being made for the holding of a bazaar, probably in August. The Bishop of Carlisle has promised to open the Institute when completed.

Soulby's Ulverston Advertiser and General Intelligencer – Thursday, June 21st 1906

MILLOM PARISH CHURCH INSTITUTE
GRAND BIZARRE IN THE DRILL HALL

A bazaar in aid of the building fund of the new Millom Parish Church Institute at present in course of erection at the lower end of Cambridge Street, Holborn Hill, was held on Wednesday and Thursday in the Drill Hall.

The Rev. Canon Irving, in opening the proceedings, said he had a double duty to perform. Not only had he to invite Mrs. Riley to open the bazaar, but he wished to thank them most heartily for their attendance there that afternoon, and in such numbers. There was no doubt but what the object for which they had gathered together, and which they all had so much at heart, would be carried through, and that the completion of their Parish Institute was sure to be accomplished. Ever since he came to Millom, over 41 years ago, the parishioners had always given their hearty support to the objects promoted by the clergy and church official, and he had no doubt that it would be so on the present occasion. He wished to thank every worker most heartily and most gratefully for the help they had given. The lady who had come to open the bazaar, Mrs. Riley, Ennin, and formerly of Broadgate, had taken a great interest in the district. Her presence there that afternoon brought old times back again. Thirty years ago or more, she was then a little girl, and took part in a similar function to that of this afternoon, but she did more work for the parish than many a big one, and the influence that she then held had not died out. Her practical sympathy in coming amongst them that afternoon was a sign that she had not forgotten her old associations. He had great pleasure in calling upon Mrs. Riley to declare the Bazaar open.

Mrs. Riley, in her opening remarks, said, Canon Irving, ladies and gentlemen, - I am sincerely obliged to Canon Irving for the delicate manner in which he referred to my early connections with the Millom Parish Church, but it would be at least 40 years since the incident happened. In coming to Millom she always felt she was coming among old friends. Although it was over a quarter of a century ago since she had left the district, she was only too pleased at any time to help forward any good work in the town. Her heart was very much in this part of the county, although she resided at a distance. When she heard that Canon Irving was going to hold a bazaar, she was only too pleased to render him any assistance, especially as the object for which they had gathered together that afternoon was for such a splendid addition to the outside influence of the church. Such institutions were a blessing to the young men of the parish. She had always realised that, and they helped to bring together young and old men in a manner which was far better than the meeting together in a public-house. She hoped when the Institute opened it would be able to open its doors free from debt, not only for the sake of the dear old Vicar, but also for the sake of the men who would use it. She had the greatest of pleasure in declaring the bazaar open – (applause).

The Millom Gazette – September 28th 1906

CANON IRVING DANGEROUSLY ILL

Very little hope is held out for the recovery of the Rev. Canon Irving, Vicar of the Millom Parish Church. He took a turn for the worse on Wednesday, and although he has rallied somewhat since, on enquiry at the vicarage this morning, we were informed his condition is the same, and is very weak. Only a week since, he took an active part in the Parish Church Institute Bazaar, and pathetically made reference to the 41 years he had spent in the parish as Vicar.

The Millom Gazette – Friday, October 5th 1906

DEATH OF CANON IRVING
FORTY-ONE YEARS VICAR OF MILLOM

The Rev. John Irving, M.A.,

HON. CANON OF CARLISLE,

VICAR OF MILLOM FROM OCT. 1865 TO OCT. 1906.

BORN JANUARY 3rd, 1831.
DIED OCTOBER 7th, 1906.

Canon Irving, vicar of Millom, passed away early yesterday morning, at his residence, Millom Vicarage. Though he has been in declining health for over 12 months, he was able to continue to take part in the work of the parish, and about a week prior to his death he presided at the opening ceremony of a bazaar in aid of the funds of a new Parish Institute. In consequence he caught a chill, which terminated fatally.

Canon Irving was an M.A. of Queen's College, Oxford. He was ordained Deacon in 1855. For a year he was Curate of Grendon, Northants, and he was perpetual Curate of Stainmore, Brough, Westmorland from

1857 to 1865, when he was appointed Vicar of Holy Trinity, Millom. He has been a Hon. Canon in Carlisle Cathedral since 1905.

Canon Irving, during his 41 years' residence in Millom, saw the town grow from the small fishing village of Holborn Hill, of 200 to 300 people, to a mining town with a population of 11,000. When he was appointed to the living at Millom, the Parish Church was the only place of worship in the district, whilst there are now no less than 16 buildings devoted to religious worship, five of them belonging to the Church of England.

When Millom was formed into a School Board district, Canon Irving was one of the members elected, and for several years occupied the position of chairman. He was one of the oldest magistrates in the Bootle Petty Sessional Division, his appointment dating back to 1870. Until declining health prevented him from doing so, he attended regularly the Millom and Bootle Police Court.

He took an active part in having three day schools built in the parish, these being handed over to the School Board when that authority was appointed.

Canon Irving was born in North Cumberland. His Grandmother was a sister of John Peel, the famous huntsman and he was able to relate many curious tales of Peel and his hunting career.

Mrs. Irving died about four years ago, and since her death the deceased never seemed to recover his worried spirits and health. He was tolerant in his views, and was highly respected by all religious bodies in Millom.

Soulby's Ulverston Advertiser and General Intelligencer – October 11th 1906

Irving family grave in Holy Trinity Churchyard

"Until the daybreak" In loving memory of Jane the beloved wife of Revd. John Irving who died July 29th 1901 aged 68 years. Laetitia Eleanor Thompson their second daughter died at Kirkby Stephen December 27th 1930 aged 56 years. Left side: Also of John Irving, Vicar of Millom for 41 years & Hon. Canon of Carlisle, who died October 7th 1906 aged 75 years. Greatly beloved. Right side: Also of Mary Isabel their dearly loved youngest daughter born November 10th 1877 died September 27th 1931 (Headstone inscription courtesy of the members of Millom Folk Museum).

FUNERAL OF CANON J. IRVING
IMPRESSIVE SCENES

On Wednesday afternoon the mortal remains of the late Canon J. Irving were laid in the burial ground of Holy Trinity Church.

The coffin had been brought from the Vicarage on Tuesday evening, and a service was held in the Church, the corpse remaining in the church, in front of the altar, all night. The service was attended by the deceased's relatives and intimate friends and the officials of the church. The Rev. L. G. Davis, M.A., officiated.

On Wednesday afternoon the interment took place. The congregation began to assemble just after 1 o'clock, and by the time the service commenced, there was not an available seat to be had, and quite a hundred had to stand, in addition when a large number could not gain admission, and had to remain on the outside of the Church. Amongst those present were:- The Hon. Mrs. Cross and Misses Cross (Ash House); the Hon. Miss Cross (Eccleriggs); Mr. and Mrs. Lewthwaite (Broadgate); Mrs. Riley (Ennin); Mr. and Mrs. C. J. Myers (Dunningwell); Mr. and Mrs. W. J. Yarr, Mrs. Ingledow, Miss Myers (Gateside); The Misses Stoney, Mr. G. Thompson (Stovers, Westmorland); Mr. G. N. Warbrick (Po House); Mr. John Newton (Ruskin Mount); Mr. T. Benn (Hestham); Mr. John Clarke (Broughton-in-Furness); Mr. J. K. Shephard (High Brow); Mr. Geo. Hill; Mr. W. B. Walker (Whicham); Mr. and Mrs. R. A. Mitchell, Mr. J. W. Brockbank, Mr. W. Crump, Mr. W. Bradley, Mr. A. J. Hutchinson; Mr. E. Brockbank (The Croft); Mr. R. G. W. Bradley; Mr. and Mrs. Knipe (The Hill); Messrs. H. F. Fox and A. F. Fox; C. A. Oglethorpe, C. Vaughan, W. I. Barratt, P. B. Stoney, W. Waite, T. Floyd, F. Mills, P. Gregson, T. H. Hodgson, W. Atkinson (Millom); Mr. and Mrs. Ewart (The Green); Rev. Geo. Postlethwaite (Vicar of St. George's, Barrow); Rev. T. Hackworth; F. Dawson and H. Shaw (Hill-of-Millom); R. Atkinson, S. Slater, Rev. J. Ninnis, Rev. Isaac Lewis, Rev. J. Kelly, Rev. H. Hartley, Messrs. J. McGowan, J. J. Cain; P. Newton (The Hawes); T. Huggins and Mrs. Huggins, T. W. H. Cartwright, J. B. Postlethwaite (Old Hall, Waberthwaite); Wm. Watson and Miss Watson (Millom Castle); T. Newby (Haverigg); J. T. Davis, W. T. Lawrence, J. Graham, J. H. Kirby, A. Shepherd, J. Shepherd, J. Trenwith, J. R. Johnson and J. Danson etc., etc.

The clergy of the diocese were represented by the following: Canon Bell (Muncaster); Rev. J. P. Haslam (Thwaites); Rev. Spurrier (Irton); Rev. J. Harrison (Waberthwaite); Rev. W. P. Ingledow (Whicham); Rev. Ivor G. Farrar (St. George's), Rev. F. Pascoe; Rev. W. Stratton (St. Luke's); Rev. W. T. Whittaker (Ulpha); Rev. J. Neale (Bootle, whilst the Rev. T. B. C. Wren, a former curate at the Holy Trinity was also present, and the Rev. H. Copinger-Hill (rector of Buxhall, Suffolk), nephew of the late Canon Irving, assisted the Rev. L. G. Davis, M.A., with the service. There were also several clergymen present who were unrobed.

The clergymen robed in the Sunday School, and proceeded to the church, being followed by the churchwardens of the Parish Church and representatives of the other churches in the town and district. St. George's sent Messrs. P. Gregson and C. A. Oglethorpe; St. Luke's: Messrs. Waite and T. Floyd; Kirksanton, Mr. T. Benn; The Hill, Mr. F. Dawson; Whicham, Mr. W. B. Walker, J.P., whilst the Holy Trinity Church officials were: Messrs. H. F. Fox and W. Watson, churchwardens; T. W. H. Cartwright and J. Trenwith, sidesmen.

The service opened with the singing of the hymn "Abide with me," after which the 90th Psalm was intoned by the Rev. L. G. Davis, followed by the reading of the 15th chap. of the first Epistle of Paul to the Corinthians by the Rev. H. Copinger-Hill. The singing of the hymn "Now the labourer's task is o'er," was feelingly sung by the choir, and afterwards the organ gradually and most dramatically broke from the hymn into the "Dead March." Many impressive scenes were witnessed, and few in the church were unaffected. Whilst the organist, Mr. Hall, was rendering the Dead March, the choir boys slowly walked from the church, followed by the elder members of the choir, and then the church official, after whom came the clergy. The coffin was then brought down the centre aisle, the bearers being: Messrs. H. F. Fox, W. Watson, T. W. H. Cartwright, F. Dawson, T. Newby and J. Trenwith.

The principle mourners followed the coffin to the graveside, they being: the three Misses Irving, Mr. and Mrs. Ley (sister-in-law); Mrs. Wynne and Mr. Dawson-Greene. The rest of the congregation followed to the place of interment, where the grave had been most beautifully decorated with white dahlias and chrysanthemums around the sides, with a layer of coloured dahlias at the bottom, upon which the coffin would lay. The grave was in the form of a vault bricked in, and all around the tops, both of the bricking and sides, Michaelmas daisies had been laid, the whole forming a pleasing site. This work had been done by the Misses Stoney and Mr. F. Futer of Dunningwell, the necessary flowers having been provided by Mrs. Myers. A beautiful cross of hot-house flowers was suspended from the tombstone of the grave of the deceased's late wife, one of the prettiest possible to see.

When the coffin arrived at the grave, the Rev. Canon Bell conducted the service, the responses being made by the clergy who had formed up round the grave, whilst the principal mourners stood at the grave side. The coffin which was of polished oak, with heavy brass fittings, was lowered into the prepared place, and the service proceeded. The singing of the Nunc Dimittis by the assembled choir, and the pronouncing of the Benediction brought the service to a close. The inscription on the coffin read:

John Irving,
Born Jan. 12th, 1831,
Died Oct. 7th, 1906

A considerable number of wreaths were received, the following being something like a complete list:-

Rev. S. Ireman, Mr. and Mrs. Ormandy, Mr. and Mrs. Trenwith, Mr. C. Vaughan, Mrs. Jenkinson (London, S.W.), Mr. and Mrs. Hockaday, Mr. and Mrs. H. F. Fox, Mr. and Mrs. Ley, Holy Trinity Men's Bible Class, Holy Trinity Choir, Holy Trinity Sunday School teachers and superintendent, Holy Trinity Sunday School scholars, Mr. and Mrs. Stoney, Mr. and Mrs. Stoner, Holy Trinity Mothers' meeting, Friends from Ash House, Mrs. Hamlet Riley (Ennin), Mrs. Hill (Buxhall, Suffolk), Mrs. C. G. Vaughan, Servants at Millom Vicarage, Mr. and Mrs. Lewthwaite (Broadgate), Mr. and Mrs. Barrett, Holy Trinity Boys' Bible Class, Mr. and Mrs. Illingworth, Mr. and Mrs. Dawson-Greene, Vicar and wardens of St. George's, Mrs. Brockbank, Mr. and Mrs. Chilson, Mrs. Sawrey-Cookson (Broughton), Mr. and Mrs. Knipe, Hill of Millom Day and Sunday School, Mrs. Singleton and Mrs. Myers.

Perhaps the most pathetic tributes were those of some of the old parishioners who brought with them bunches of home grown flowers and deposited them near the grave and upon the coffin.

When the coffin was lowered into the grave it was noticed that the surplice, hood and stole were lowered also. These were gifts of the parishioners to the late Canon Irving on his having attained 40 years as Vicar of Holy Trinity. After the service was concluded they were brought up, and will be prized very highly by the relatives.

The funeral arrangements were in the hands of Mr. A. Birbeck of Holborn Hill.

The church had been draped in a beautiful manner by Mr. J. R. Johnston, and hymn sheets were provided. The whole of the arrangements went off without an incident, everything having been arranged in an excellent manner by the Rev. L. G. Davis, the churchwardens, Mr. W. Watson, H. F. Fox and the other officials of the church. No pains were spared to accommodate everyone who assembled to pay their last respects to the late Canon and the officials deserve praise for the manner in which the whole ceremony was carried out.

The Millom Gazette – Friday, October 12th 1906

THE MILLOM VICARIATE

We understand that the Rev. C. Whittaker, perpetual Vicar of Ulpha, has been offered, and has accepted the Vicariate of Millom.

The Millom Gazette – Friday, November 23rd 1906

THE VICARIATE OF MILLOM

We are authorised to make the following announcement concerning the resignation of the Rev. C. Whittaker, from the Vicariate of Millom: - "Holy Trinity, Millom: The Rev. Chas. Whittaker, on further consideration of the Bishop's offer to him of the benefice of Holy Trinity, Millom, has decided to withdraw his acceptance of the offer, and this will enable him to continue some extra parochial duties for the Church, such as honorary work for the Waifs and Strays and the Navvy Mission Society."

The Millom Gazette – Friday, December 14th 1906

LOCAL NOTES
THE VACANT VACARIATE

The fact that the Rev. Charles Whittaker, after having accepted the benefice of Holy Trinity has, on further consideration, decided to withdraw his acceptance of the Vicariate is further proof that great difficulty will most certainly be encountered in filling the vacant office. When all facts are taken into consideration, it is not surprising that this is the case, as the living is by no means a "fat" one, seeing that the stipend amounts to only £230, and out of this, it is essential that in addition to a curate, extraneous aid is needed, and has to be paid for. In addition to the work in connection with the Holy Trinity Church, and this by itself is no light matter, services at Kirksanton and The Hill have to be held and then the large Bible Class and Sunday School, and the Holborn Hill Mission Hall all call for further labour, so that it is absolutely impossible for one to do all that is necessary. On the face of it, it is decidedly out of the question for one person to be in three places at once, and on Sundays, seeing that three services are being held at one and the same time, it is essential that help must be called in. The late Canon Irving, after having paid for the assistance it was necessary for him to have, had something like £10 left after paying out all the expenses paid yearly.

Certainly there a societies which provide a sufficient sum to pay a curate, and the need of one in the parish of Holy Trinity should be sufficient to justify an application for help in this direction. The main object, first of all, however, is to get the office filled as quickly as possible, and seeing that we have near at home one, at least, who would fill the position, knowing, as he does, the requirements of the parish, it would seem unnecessary to go further afield. Rumour has many tongues, and the report was current that the living has again been accepted, but we are not in a position to give particulars that might be accepted with confidence. As the matter stands at present it is very unpleasant all round, and the sooner some solution to the problem of providing Millom with a vicar is solved, the more satisfactory it will be to all concerned.

The Millom Gazette – Friday, December 14th 1906

1907

VICAR OF MILLOM APPOINTED

We are able to announce that the office of Vicar of Millom has finally been accepted, and the new Vicar is the Rev. W. Kewley, Vicar of Natland, near Kendal.

Old residents will remember that Mr. Kewley acted as curate under the late Canon Irving from 1876 to 1881, and that during the time he resided in Millom, he identified himself with every movement of local interest.

In 1881 he accepted the Vicariate of Ulpha, and did good service in that out-of-the-way parish until 1897, when he exchanged livings with the Rev. C. Whittaker, who is at present Vicar of Ulpha, and who, a few weeks ago, declined to accept the Vicariate of Millom.

The Rev. W. Kewley is a Theological Associate of King's College, London, and was ordained deacon in 1876, the curacy of Holy Trinity being his first office.

The present stipend of the Vicar of Natland is £233, and a parsonage, the population being a scattered one, and only numbering 553. The income of the Vicar of Holy Trinity is £228, and parsonage, and the living is solely in the presentation of the Bishop of Carlisle. The population of Holy Trinity Parish is 2,963, whilst that of St. George's Parish is 8,300.

It is expected that the Rev. gentleman will take up the duties in a short time, and the parishioners who know Mr. Kewley personally, are hoping to again welcome him to the parish with which he is so well acquainted. The choice is a happy one in many ways, and Mr. Kewley may be relied upon to fill the office, which has now been vacant for over four months, in a manner that will give satisfaction to all concerned.

The Millom Gazette – Friday, January 11th 1907

REV. W. KEWLEY.
The Newly-appointed Vicar of Millom.

THE NEW VICAR OF MILLOM

With the current issue of the "Gazette" we have pleasure in presenting a fine art supplement of the photo of the new Vicar of Millom, who was inducted to the living of Holy Trinity on Tuesday last, by Archdeacon Campbell. Mr. Kewley is no stranger to Millom, and is fully acquainted with all the needs and demands of the parish over which he will have spiritual control. We have no doubt but what Mr. Kewley will soon be thoroughly at home in his new sphere, and before long everything in connection with the parish of Holy Trinity will resume its former activity, which, owing to the several changes since the death of the late Canon Irving, has been without a resident clergyman. As Archdeacon Campbell stated, the induction of the Rev. W. Kewley to the parish marks a new chapter in the history of the Holy Trinity Church, and we trust that the coming years, during which the rev. gentleman will labour amongst us, will be marked with brightness and success. No doubt it will be some time before the new Vicar becomes thoroughly acquainted with the large number of parishioners committed to his charge, but as the late Vicar came to be loved, respected and honoured by every inhabitant of Millom, so also will the present Vicar be blessed with the same tokens as he becomes better known.

The Millom Gazette – Friday, March 15th 1907

THE CANON IRVING MEMORIAL PORCH

By the courtesy of the committee who have the arrangements for the above Memorial in hand we are able to reproduce a sketch of the proposed memorial. At a public meeting held about the end of last year, it was unanimously decided to erect a memorial of some kind as a token of affection and esteem in which the parishioners of Holy Trinity held the late Vicar who for over 40 years ministered amongst them, and endeared himself to all. Although it was not definitely decided at that time what shape the Memorial should take, the matter has been well considered since, and the Committee have resolved that the suggestion which was made with reference to the erection of a porch at the north side of the Old Church was one which would materially increase the comfort and warmth of the church, and at the same time add to its appearance. The proposed memorial, which it is estimated, will cost about £250, is one which will meet with the approval of all, and it is well-known that the late Canon Irving would have given the undertaking his hearty support.

The committee, in soliciting subscriptions, point out that they desire to make the memorial as representative as possible, not only of the late Vicar's parishioners, but also of his personal friends. Subscriptions may be forwarded to the Rev. W. Kewley, Vicar of Millom, or to any of the banks in Millom or their local branches. The Chairman of the Committee is Dr. Butler Stoney. Mr. G. H. Scott is the hon. Secretary and treasurer, and the committee is composed of the following: Rev. W. Kewley, Messrs. H. F. fox, F. Dawson, H. J. Kirby, R. A. Mitchell, Jas. Newton, W. Watson, T. H. Dobson, J. Graham, J. Ormandy, G. H. Scott, John Shepherd, Mrs. Trenwith, Miss B. Newton, Miss Watson and Miss Stoney.

The Millom Gazette – Friday, May 3rd 1907

MILLOM PARISH CHURCH INSTITUTE
GRAND OPENING BY MISS IRVING
FASHIONABLE GATHERING

MISS IRVING

Who performed the Opening Ceremony at the Holy Trinity New Parochial Institute on Monday last.

The late Canon Irving, when he presided at the Bazaar in the Drill Hall in September last, held for the purpose of obtaining additional funds towards the building of a Parish Institute at Holborn Hill, said that there was no doubt that the object they had in view would be accomplished, namely, the completion of the building. This was the Canon's last public appearance, and less than a month afterwards, the inhabitants of Millom were mourning his death. The late Canon did much for the parish of Holy Trinity during his variate of 41 years, and the last deed of public importance he was responsible for was the commencement of a scheme for the erection of a parish institute. Unfortunately, Canon Irving did not live to see the consummation of his plans, and in consequence the proceedings at the opening of the Holy Trinity Parish Institute on Monday evening was marked by a feeling of sympathy.

Thanks to the generosity of the Hodbarrow Mining Company, who gave a subscription of £100, the bazaar, which realised over £150, and generous subscriptions from local gentry, the money at present in hand towards the estimated cost of £600 amounts to about £400. It was first thought when the proposal was first made that a building might be used as an institute in Holborn Hill, but as this was not found possible, it was decided to build a new one, and the building which was formally opened on Monday evening by Miss Irving is the result.

There was a large gathering present in the large room, when the Rev. W. Kewley, Vicar of Millom, took the chair, being supported on the platform by the Rev. L. G. Davis, Messrs. W. Watson, H. F. Fox, F. Mudge, and Miss Irving.

The Rev. W. Kewley, in opening, said that before they could proceed any further they must have the room opened. He did not know where they (the audience) were, but they could not be in the room, as it was not yet opened (laughter). He had the greatest of pleasure in asking Miss Irving to perform that ceremony (applause).

Miss Irving, who was received with great applause, was dressed in deep mourning. She said it gave her the greatest of pleasure to be present that evening in order to perform the opening ceremony. There were two qualifications, however, which were necessary for a person to possess in order to perform such a function, but which were lacking in it. One was that the person called upon should be a person of importance, and the other, that a speech should be made. "I claim," said Miss Irving, amidst applause, "to stand second to none in the interest I take in this Institute." It was in connection with the preliminary work of that Institute that her dear father had made his last public appearance, and for that reason alone it would always have their greatest support. Two words could be written large with regard to the beautiful building they were in, and they were: generosity and enthusiasm – generosity of the friends and enthusiasm of the workers (applause). Those two qualities always stood out so far as the inhabitants of Millom were concerned. This was the first time she had been in the building, and she could only say how delighted she was to see such a beautiful place. She hoped that all the recreation which took place in the building would prove to be for the glory of God and the good of the parish (applause). In declaring the Institute open, Miss Irving hoped that it would meet with every success (prolonged applause).

The Chairman then handed Miss Irving a beautiful silver key as a souvenir of the opening of the building which Miss Irving has spoken so appropriately.

Miss Irving, in accepting the key, said it was most delightful, as it would always remind her of her friends in Millom, and she assured them that her friendship should remain as bright and shining as she would keep the key. On behalf of her sisters and herself she had pleasure in handing to Mr. F. Mudge a framed photograph of her father, which she hoped would hang upon a wall of the building (applause).

The Rev. W. Kewley, in a sincere manner, paid a fitting tribute to the memory of the late Canon Irving, who, said the rev. gentleman, was far more capable of presiding at a gathering of that character than he. Everybody would feel gratified at the work which had been carried out, and they all felt grateful to him who had been responsible for the beginning of the building of the Institute, and who was called away before its completion. As the late Canon Irving had often said, it was not always that the fruits of one's labour could be seen, but that God should receive the benefit. One of the great needs in the past had been a room in which the Bible Class could be held, and where the members could meet together for spiritual and social intercourse. Their Bible Class was an organization consisting of, in round figures, 150, who were men – Englishmen, who met together to glorify God. It was something to be proud of. He believed that all who had taken an interest in the building of the Institute would be credited with it in the great book which would be opened hereafter. He believed that the Institute would be a power for good in the parish.

The Millom Gazette – May 10th 1907

TO MASONS AND BUILDERS

Tenders are invited for the erection of a porch to the principle door of the Parish Church, Millom. Plans and specifications may be seen after the 10th inst., on application to the undersigned.

Tenders endorsed "Porch" to be sent in not later than the 24th inst. The lowest or any tender not necessarily accepted.

G. H. Scott,
Hon. Secretary to the Committee,
10, Victoria Street,
Millom.

The Millom Gazette – July 12th 1907

TRAGIC DEATH OF THE VICAR OF MILLOM

KILLED WHILST HAYMAKING

DEATH NOTICE

KEWLEY.- On July 10th, suddenly at Millom Vicarage, result of an accident, the Rev. Wm. Kewley, Vicar of Millom, aged 55 years.

Interment to-morrow (Saturday), at the Parish Church, at 1 p.m.

The Millom Gazette – Friday, July 12th 1907

Quite a sensation was caused in Millom and district on Wednesday evening, when the news was circulated to the effect that the Rev. William Kewley, vicar of Holy Trinity, had been killed. The news spread rapidly, and a large number of people stirred by curiosity, at once made their way to the scene of the accident.

It appears that the Rev. and Mrs. Kewley had invited a number of church workers to tea on the Vicarage lawn on Wednesday afternoon previous to which the majority engaged in hay-making in the field below the Vicarage. The day was beautifully fine, and the party thoroughly enjoyed themselves, little thinking that their happiness was so soon to be marred by such a shocking accident as that which occurred between 6.30 and 7 o'clock. After tea the Church workers, along with Mrs. Kewley and the Misses Kewley, commenced playing croquet, and other games on the lawn, whilst Mr. Kewley, along with two of the female servants and two other men, went into the field, which is very steep, and commenced to load the hay that was ready.

One half of the field had been mown, and the greater part of the hay stacked, that at the bottom end of the field, however, not having been cut for a distance of about 30 yards from the hedge. A girl named Grace Dixon was leading the pony and cart between the rows, and experienced no difficulty in managing it. Mr. Kewley and one of the men were forking the hay on to the cart, and James Boow, the gardener, was placing it. The girl leading the pony was told to lead it up higher and in doing so the pony, it is supposed, slipped. The pony's head at the time was uphill, but it became excited, and finally turned round. The weight of the cart and hay was too heavy for the pony to hold, and it commenced to run downhill. The girl Dixon endeavoured to hold it, but could not do so, Mr. Kewley, seeing the evident danger of the man and girl, ran to their assistance, his intention undoubtedly being to turn the animal's head round in order to stay its downward progress, but in this he was not successful, unfortunately, and it is assumed that he was knocked down, and the cart wheel ran over his chest. The man Boow, who was on the top of the hay when the pony commenced to gallop, jumped off, and did not see the accident, and beyond the supposition that the cart wheel did go over deceased's chest, nothing further can be stated on this point.

Dr. Stoney was at once sent for, and the melancholy news spread so fast that practically everyone was in possession of the supposed facts of the case. When the medical man arrived the unfortunate gentleman had breathed his last, and only spoke once after the accident. Mrs. Kewley and her daughters were at once informed, and found their husband and father lying unconscious. Miss Bell, Mrs. W. Hutchinson, and Mrs. W. Dixon were at hand, but all their efforts to restore consciousness were unavailing, but twenty minutes passed before he passed away. A slight wound on the deceased's forehead was noticeable, but beyond this, no outward injuries were seen, and it is supposed that death occurred from internal haemorrhage.

Only a quarter of an hour before the accident, deceased was chatting quite gaily on the lawn with several of the workers, and discussing details with reference to the annual treat, which would have been held on the 24th inst., but which has now been postponed.

The Rev. William Kewley was a Theological Associate of King's College, London, was ordained in 1896, and accepted the curacy of Holy Trinity Church in the same year under the late Canon Irving. He held this office until 1881, when he accepted the Vicariate of Ulpha, and during his connection with that out-of-the-way parish he worked hard for the benefit of the parishioners. In 1897 he exchanged livings with the Rev. C. Whittaker, the present Vicar of Ulpha, and up to March 12th of this year, remained at Natland, near Kendal. Those with whom he came in contact in that parish speak most highly of his services, and the news of his sudden demise will be received with the same expressions of regret that have been heard on every hand in Millom since the sad and painful accident. His popularity amongst the parishioners when he acted as curate has been further enhanced during the four months he has filled the office of Vicar, and the enthusiastic manner in which he had entered into the work of the parish has endeared him to all. Arrangements had been made with the Rev. W. P. Ingledow, Rector of Whicham, to assist him in the religious work, and a mid-week evening service was being held in the Parish Room when the news arrived that the Vicar had been killed. The Rev. W. P. Ingledow at once stopped the service and proceeded to the Vicarage.

In the first Holy Trinity parish magazine organised by Mr. Kewley and which was issued this month appeared his first letter to his parishioners.

Deceased was 55 years of age, and leaves a widow and a family of four – three daughters and one son.

THE INQUEST

was held in the dining room at the Millom Vicarage yesterday (Thursday) afternoon, before Dr. P. B. Stoney, coroner, and the following jury: Messrs. Thos. Taylor Tyson (Low House), John Newton (Waterblean), T. H. Hodgson (Salthouse), W. H. Kitchen and H. Airey (Hawbank), T. H. Huggins, E. Griffin, P. Gregson, T. H. Cartwright, C. Walmsley, T. Dowell and W. Tyson.

Mr. P. Gregson was chosen as foreman of the jury, and after the body had been viewed, the first witness called was Joseph Boow, who said he lived at Hawbank, and was a groom and gardener at the Millom Vicarage. He identified the body viewed by the jury as that of William Kewley; of the Vicarage.

He was working in the field with the deceased on Wednesday afternoon. Witness was loading hay on the cart, but they were all making hay. William Crouthers and Harry Singleton were forking, and deceased was raking with the big rake. Grave Dixon, one of the aids, was leading the horse up the hill when the cart was half loaded. The horse became excited and seemed to turn down the hill.

The Coroner: Was the load too heavy for her? – I don't think so. The horse turned down the hill, but I could hardly see, being on top of the cart.

Witness said he leapt off the cart when he saw something was wrong, and when he got up he saw the horse half way down the hill, and the deceased was holding the reins close to the horse's head. Deceased then fell.

The Coroner: Did he leave go, or did he fall? – I cannot say; he seemed to fall.

Did he trip up in the long grass? – Yes, I think that was the reason of his falling. The cart seemed to go over his ribs.

Which way was he lying? – It was that quick I can hardly tell you.

Did he sit up afterwards? – No, he moved a bit, but he never sat up. The cart seemed to have gone over his chest. Deceased never spoke to witness after the occurrence.

The Foreman: Was the pony galloping down the hill? – It was going very quickly; the cart seemed to be running over the horse.

By the Foreman: It was not the shaft that appeared to knock deceased down.

Grace Dixon, who was evidently greatly affected, said she was a housemaid and lived at the Vicarage. She was out haymaking on Wednesday afternoon, along with the other servant and the gardener and a couple of men. She was raking the hay I rows until they came down with the horse. It was the first time she had ever led that horse. Witness was told to lead it up the field and did so, and after leading her so far, the horse went down on its knees; its head was uphill at the time, and it then reared up and turned down the hill, starting to gallop. Witness kept hold of the reins until Mr. Kewley came and they both ran about three yards down the field and witness then let go. She could not hold on any longer, the horse being too strong for her. She did not find any difficulty with the grass. The cart did not go very far after she let go – perhaps 20 yards – (pointing to some trees out on the lawn: "So far.") Mr. Kewley held on for some time, and witness saw him fall. She did not know whether the cart went over the deceased or not. Witness then ran down with Mr. Singleton and took deceased's collar off. Deceased never spoke. Witness stayed two or three minutes, and she then went for assistance.

By the Coroner: Deceased never said anything while witness was there. Mrs. Kewley was just coming down as witness went up for some brandy.

Was he moved at all from where he fell? – No, sir.

By the Foreman: Witness was not there when Mr. Kewley died.

By Inspector Dickson: A doctor was sent for at once.

By the Coroner: She did not know whether deceased was dead when the doctor arrived.

Joseph Boow (recalled) said he was present when Mr. Kewley died. A doctor was first of all sent for, but deceased had died a few minutes before the arrival of the medical man.

By the foreman: He did not hear him speak.

Mr. Walmsley: Was the horse not a mettlesome one? – No.

The Coroner: The girl said the horse reared up and came down on his knees. – Well, I can hardly say, sir, as I was on the top of the cart. She might have fancied that the horse had come down on its knees, but so far as I know, the horse slipped.

The Coroner: if it fell on its knees it could not recover itself again.

By a juryman: Oh, yes, I have often seen horses get up after going on their knees.

This was all the evidence.

A juryman said he was present at the time Mr. Kewley spoke. He only said, "My God, my God! Is the doctor coming?"

The Coroner said it was a very sad affair, but there seemed no doubt that it was an accident. A mark on deceased's head was only just a scratch. It was not material in any case, but the question was, "How did the thing happen?" The evidence of the witness Boow showed that the horse ran away.

A verdict of "Accidental Death" was returned.

At the conclusion of the inquest, the foreman, Mr. Gregson, proposed a vote of heartfelt sympathy to Mrs. Kewley and the family in their terrible bereavement, and said in the few weeks he had been amongst them he had won all hearts, and in many houses the good he had done would never pass away. It was wonderful to think how anyone could in so short a time have so completely won the hearts of his parishioners.

Mr. Griffin seconded, and said as a member of a neighbouring church, he endorsed all the foreman had said, and he believed the feeling of the parish was as if there had been a personal loss.

The Coroner, in thanking the jury, and promising to convey their resolution to Mrs. Kewley, said that Mr. Kewley was his oldest friend, and that when he knew he was coming to Millom he had said, "I am not coming to a new parish, but I am coming home, doctor."

The Millom Gazette – Friday, July 12th 1907

THE LATE VICAR OF MILLOM
FUNERAL ON SATURDAY LAST
LARGE GATHERING

William Kewley grave in Holy Trinity Churchyard

"In loving memory of William Kewley aged 55 years, Vicar of Millom from March 9th to July 10th 1907. "And he was not for God took him." Also of Margaret Binnie his wife who died January 31st 1934 aged 84 years. Left side: Also of his only son, William Christopher (Kit), killed in action at St. Eloi April 13th 1916 aged 24 years"

Amidst every manifestation of sympathy and sorrow the interment of the late Rev. William Kewley took place at Holy Trinity Churchyard. There was a considerable number of parishioners and others present, but the weather conditions accounted for the fact that a large gathering was not present. Rain fell throughout the morning, and about the time the cortege left the Millom Vicarage it was pouring down heavily. It continued raining until the interment took place.

The old church was filled with a sympathetic congregation of mourners, and on every side could be seen marks of respect shown by the late Vicar's friends. Whilst the church was being filled, the organist, Mr. J. Hall, rendered, "Oh rest in the Lord," and then followed the opening hymn, "Thy will be done." Psalm 39: "I said I would heed of my ways," was read by the Rev. J. Casson, of Leicester, the clerk and congregation making the responses. Then following the reading of the 15th chapter of St. Paul's epistle to the Corinthians, commencing at the 15th verse. The hymn, "Oh! God our help in ages past," was followed by the Lord's Prayer and the prayers for the burial of the dead. The hymn, "The King of Love my Shepherd is" brought the service in the church to a close, and whilst the organist impressively rendered the Dead March in "Saul," the coffin was carried to the graveside by the bearers. The remainder of the service was conducted by the Rev. J. P. Haslam and Ven. Archdeacon Campbell.

The chief mourners included:- Wm. C. Kewley (son); Miss Kewley, Miss E. Kewley and Miss F. Kewley (daughters); Mr. and Mrs. Mellor (sister), Mr. and Miss Bartholomew, Mr. Wilkie, Mr. J. R. Kewley, Mr. J. Mellor, jun., Rev H. Mellor, Mr. and Mrs. J. R. Hall, representatives of Natland Mothers' Meeting and churchwardens, and many other parishioners, Churchwardens and parishioners from Ulpha.

The clergy present were: Archdeacon Campbell, Barrow; Canon Bell, Muncaster; Canon Monnington, Broughton in Furness; Rev. Ivor G. Farrar, Rev. F. Pascoe, St. George's; Rev. J. P. Haslam, Thwaites; Rev W. P. Ingledow, Whicham; Rev. J. Casson, Leicester; Rev. T. Banks, Whitbeck; Rev. R. Ellwood, Torver;

Rev. K. M. Pughe, Drigg; Rev. H. Mellor (nephew); Rev. W. Whittaker, Ulpha; Rev. J. Park, Woodland; Rev. J. Neale, Bootle; Rev. Stephens, St. John's, Barrow; Rev. Ridley, Ireleth-in-Furness; Rev. J. Ninnis, Millom Bible Christians; Rev. H. Hartley, Millom Wesleyans and the Rev. S. K. Chesworth, Millom Primitive Methodists.

The bearers were: Messrs. W. Watson, W. T. H. Cartwright, F. Dawson, T. T. Tyson, T. Holmes and J. Newton (Waterblean), H. Kirby, J. Graham, H. Jenkinson, G. H. Scott, John Fisher and H. Shaw.

The grave is situated in the same part of the churchyard as that where the late Canon Irving was laid to rest. The grave had been appropriately decorated with ivy and roses, this work having been done by Miss Sykes, Miss Watson and Mr. Futer, Dunningwell. During the time the service was being read at the graveside, it rained heavily. Wreaths of a beautiful character were in abundance, and a large carriage had to be requisitioned in order to convey these floral tributes of sympathy and respect from the Vicarage to the Church.

A large number of parishioners laid bunches of flowers on the grave on Sunday, these being more numerous than the wreaths and larger tributes.

The Millom Gazette – Friday, July 19th 1907

THE LATE REV. WM. KEWLEY

A public meeting in connection with the Millom Parish Church was held in the Mission Room, Holborn Hill, on Thursday evening last to take into consideration the question of raising funds for a memorial to the late Vicar. The Rev. J. P. Haslam, Vicar of Thwaites, presided over a well-attended meeting which was unanimously in favour of the proposition. The following ladies and gentlemen were elected as the committee, Mrs. Fox, Misses Bell, Stable, Watson and Newton. Messrs. W. Barratt, W. T. H. Cartwright, F. Dawson, T. H. Dobson, H. F. Fox, J. Graham, P. Gregson, Rev. J. P. Haslam, H. J. Kirby, R. Lindsay, H. Mansfield, R. A. Mitchell, T. J. Newby, J. Ormandy, J. Shepherd, C. Stephenson, P. B. Stoney, C. Vaughan and W. Watson with Mr. G. H. Scott as hon. secretary.

We understand that the committee will get to work at once to carry out the proposition put forward. Friends or parishioners desiring to help us to associate themselves with any of the committee or the hon. secretary, whose address is 10, Victoria Street, Millom.

The Millom Gazette – Friday, September 6th 1907

NEW VICAR OF HOLY TRINITY

The Rev. R. S. G. Green, M.A., who has been appointed Vicar of Millom, is the second son of the late Rev. J. H. Green, M.A., formerly rector of Croglin, and received his education at Queen's College, Oxford, where he was elected a Hastings Exhibitor in 1884, and from where he graduated in 1888 with second-class honours in Literae Humaniores, having previously been placed in the second class in Moderations in 1886. In 1889, Mr. Green was ordained deacon by the Bishop of Barrow-in-Furness, and became curate of St. Mary's, Ulverston, where he remained two years until in 1891 he was presented to the family living of Croglin, which is now in the gift of his brother , Mr. L. H. M. Green. Mr. Green married in 1900, Margaret Helen, eldest daughter of Mr. John Sowerby, of Newcastle-on-Tyne, and granddaughter of the late Mr. John Sowerby, of Benwell Tower, Northumberland.

For the last nine years Mr. Green has been a member of the Penrith Rural District Council and Board of Guardians as the representative of Croglin.

The Millom Gazette – Friday, September 27th 1907

THE INSTITUTION TO HOLY TRINITY

The new Vicar of Holy Trinity Church – Rev. R. S. G. Green – was instituted to the living by the Bishop of Carlisle on Saturday last, and we understand his induction takes place next week, and will be performed by the Archdeacon of Furness. It is hardly necessary to say that Mr. Green will take his position as Vicar with the heartiest and best wishes of the whole of the people of Millom. Holy Trinity parish has had a chequered history of late, but it is confidently anticipated that with the advent of a comparatively young

Vicar, there will be new life infused into the affairs of the parish. The only wonder is that with the vacancies that have existed of late, the Church should still retain such a hold upon the affections of the people as it undoubtedly does, and this fact says much for the zeal with which parochial affairs must have been attended to by Church officials during the recent interregnums. We hope they may witness still greater in the future.

The Millom Gazette – Friday, October 25th 1907

INDUCTION CEREMONY AT THE HOLY TRINITY CHURCH

The induction of the Rev. R. S. G. Green to Holy Trinity Church, took place on Monday evening in the presence of a large congregation. The ceremony was performed by the Ven. H. E. Campbell, Archdeacon of Furness, the other clergy present and taking part in the service being: Revs. Ivor G. Farrar (Vicar of St. George's, Millom), Rev. W. P. Ingledow (Rector of Whicham), Rev. J. P. Haslam (Vicar of Thwaites and Rev. Watson Stratton (St. Luke's, Haverigg).

In his address, the Ven. Archdeacon said: The circumstances connected with the holding of this service tonight are unusually solemn and pathetic. This is the second time this year that it has been my duty, as your Archdeacon, to come and induct a new Vicar of this parish, and to give him a welcome to this place, and to offer prayer for him, to witness his undertaking the duties of this cure, and to unite in solemn prayer to God, and to promise to help him in this place. Now, unlike Mr. Kewley, Mr. Green comes to you as a stranger – a stranger both to you and me – though not entirely a stranger in this district. He is sent here by the Bishop, who is the patron of this living, and I am fully confident that the Bishop in this appointment, has given very careful consideration before he arrived at the decision, and before taking action and sending a man here to this cure, because I am sure that he, knowing the special circumstances of this parish, has made it a special matter of prayer and consideration, and his one and only object in appointing a Vicar to Millom has been to find in the diocese the most suitable man in his opinion to discharge the duties of this office. Mr. Green has had experience in an agricultural parish, he has had experience and lived amongst those who are cultivating the soil; he will know their ways, their thoughts, their feelings, their tastes, their temptations; he will be able, I think, to work in sympathy with them, and readily understand their ways, and will soon be able to make himself thoroughly at home with the people who are engaged in this kind of occupation in this parish. Moreover, he has been working in a parish in Cumberland, so there is no need to tell him that Cumberland people like first, when a stranger comes, to get to know him for a time before they give him their entire confidence and sympathy, but when they do give it they give it with all their heart: it is a steadfast faith and a true allegiance that they give to the man who they feel is a true man, ever ready with human kindliness to go in and out amongst them in humility, love and sympathy, to live as a brother and friend amongst them. And when they find out that a man sets before him a very high ideal of his holy calling and strives to declare the Word of God with zeal and earnestness and to lead people into righteousness, and when they see that his life corresponds with his word and he is devoted to his calling and full of love to his people, then I think the people of Cumberland are very ready to embrace that man in their hearts, and to revere, trust and follow him as a true and faithful guide and friend. I trust, then, that all this will be fulfilled. Do not suppose I am saying that a clergyman is coming in the parish simply to win the esteem and popularity of the people. Far otherwise! We would be less than human if we did not esteem your faith and appreciation, and your love. It is right that we should do so, but we have far other things to do than this. We have to try to lead you into holiness, to declare more fully the will of God, to give His message to the people, to urge them to depart from sin and to follow Christ. Now, this evening Mr. Green is going to be inducted to this living, and these same solemn promises made in the sight of God, that were entered upon by our departed friend, will be made by him this evening in your presence. You will all witness how he undertakes his solemn duties and responsibilities. I ask you, who are not called upon to make promises, I call upon you, brethren, all, after this extraordinary time of trial, to be united together in holy love and fellowship, to support him. These bereavements, these losses, disappointments, and long delay, all this been extremely unsettling. But you are about to make a fresh start again to-night. Seek to renew your energy, to have fresh consecrated devotion, to be a living, powerful Church in this place for the good of souls and the benefit of the people. Pray unto God for your new minister, and help him forward in all the work that he undertakes in this place, to the glory of God and the benefit of Christ's people.

The Millom Gazette – Friday, November 1st 1907

1908

MEMORIAL WINDOW TO THE LATE CANON AND MRS. IRVING

From the Holy Trinity Magazine we gather that at the last meeting of the Consistory Court in Carlisle a faculty was issued for the insertion of a window in Millom Parish Church to the memory of the late Canon and Mrs. Irving. The window is being put in by the Misses Irving, from a design by Messrs. Shrigley & Hunt, and it is hoped that it may be finished in time to be dedicated during the service on Whit Sunday evening.

The Millom Gazette – Friday, June 5th 1908

Irving Memorial window at Holy Trinity Church . Image © Bry Cooper

"To the Glory of God & in loving memory of John Irving M.A. died Oct. 7th 1906 and of Jane Irving died July 29th 1901 this window is inserted by their daughters"

DEDICATION OF STAINED GLASS WINDOW AT MILLOM PARISH CHURCH

The beautiful stained glass window, in memory of the late Canon and Mrs. Irving, was dedicated by the Rev. R. S. G. Green (vicar). It was sent here complete, and the work of inserting it took only one day. The figures are representative of the Virgin Mary and St. John, the effect being very beautiful. The Vicar said a short Dedicatory prayer, and in the course of his sermon, briefly referred to Canon Irving's labours in the parish, and the benefits of his 40 years' ministry, He also commented upon the many changes the parish had gone through in that time.

The window, which is outside the Chancel, has two lights, and has been erected by the daughters of the late Canon Irving. There was a large congregation.

The Millom Gazette – Friday, June 12th 1908

Rev. William Kewley Memorial tablet in Holy Trinity Church. Image © Bry Cooper

IN MEMORY OF THE LATE REV. W. KEWLEY

A short service will be held on Sunday afternoon, at half-past two o'clock, in the Millom Parish Church, to dedicate the brass tablet erected by parishioners and friends in memory of the late Vicar, the Rev. W. Kewley. The service will be conducted by the Rev. J. P. Haslam, Vicar of Thwaites.

The Millom Gazette – Friday, June 12th 1908

IN MEMORY OF THE LATE VICAR OF MILLOM

A large congregation assembled in the Parish Church on Sunday afternoon, when the Rev. J. P. Haslam of Thwaites, conducted an impressive memorial service to commemorate the death of the Rev. Wm. Kewley, who was tragically killed twelve months ago. The members of the Young Men's Bible Class attended in large numbers. A suitable form of service was gone with, appropriate hymns were sung and the Rev. J. P. Haslam eulogised the late Vicar and spoke of his sterling qualities.

The Millom Gazette – Friday, June 19th 1908

1909

Holy Trinity Church c.1909. Image reproduced here courtesy of Mrs. A. Norman

PARISH CHURCH ITEMS

We take the following paragraphs from the Millom Parish Church Magazine for the current month:-

The Rev. J. H. Watson, B.A., until recently curate of Cleator Moor, will take up work as curate of the Parish Church on January 1st. Mr. Watson, since his ordination five years ago, has worked continuously in this Diocese, and comes to us with the Bishop's express approval. The parishioners will, we are sure, offer Mr. and Mrs. Watson a hearty welcome

The Millom Gazette – Friday, January 8th 1909

1911

MILLOM CURATE'S SUICIDE

A painful sensation was created at Millom on Saturday night when it became known that the Rev. J. H. Watson, curate of Millom Parish Church, had committed suicide by hanging. Mr. Watson, who had been resident in Millom for two and a half years, had resigned his position on account of indifferent health, and at the recent vestry meeting the Vicar (Rev. R. S. G. Green) spoke highly of his work since he had been in Millom. The deceased gentleman appeared in his usual health on Saturday morning, and on seeing his wife off by train to Whitehaven, appeared to be unusually bright and cheerful. He should have met her off the mail train in the evening, but failed to do so. Mrs. Watson effected an entrance into the house at the back, and searched the premises without finding the deceased. Finding the back kitchen door locked, she called in the police, who discovered Mr. Watson hanging by some webbing from a beam. The body was at once cut down, and artificial respiration tried, but on arrival of a doctor life was pronounced to be extinct.

INQUEST

An inquest was held on Monday morning at the Police Station before Dr. Stoney, Coroner, and the following jury:- Messrs. P. Gregson, C. A. Haynes, A. R. Hudson, R. G. W. Bradley, J. H. Key, A. J. McGowan, A. Coward, J. McGuire, J. Morgan, J. W. Stoddart and E. J. Dixon.

Mr. Gregson was chosen as foreman.

Mary Catherine Watson said she lived at Duke Street, Millom, and identified the body viewed as that of her husband, John Harry Watson, who was 40 years of age, and lived with her at the above address. He was a clerk in holy orders and was curate at Millom Parish Church. Witness last saw him alive on Millom Railway Station on Saturday last at about 11.45, when he was seeing her off by train to Whitehaven. She was to return at 8.26, and expected deceased to be at the station to meet her. He was not there, and witness was disappointed, as deceased said he would be there. She went to the front door of their house and knocked, but got no answer. There was only deceased in the house. Witness then went round to the back door, put her hand through an opening in the door, and drew back the bolt on the inside. She went into the house and called for deceased, but got no answer. Witness's niece said, "Try if he is outside," and witness found the outside door fastened, so that she could not get into the back kitchen. She then went for Inspector Thwaites, and he came and burst the door open. He then said, "Run for the doctor," and witness did so. On returning, she found her husband lying on the flaggings in the back yard and the Inspector and the doctor examining him.

The Coroner: What did you do? – I went into the house, sir.

Did you know then that he was dead? – Yes, sir.

Did he have any letters or papers of any kind addressed to you or anyone? – Nothing.

Did you look for them? – Yes.

Can you give the jury any reasonable explanation why he should do this? – I cannot, unless that he used to worry very much about his work, and then he was run down a good deal.

Has he been attended by a doctor lately? – No, not lately.

Since when, this year? – No, I do not think so but he was never strong, and he was troubled about leaving Millom, and one thing and another.

But he need not have left Millom unless he liked? – No, I think not. We were talking about our future life on the station, and he seemed very bright and cheerful when I left him.

You know no reason why he should have done as he did? – No.

The Foreman: Has he seemed in low spirits lately? – No, not at all. I have not seen him so bright and cheerful as he was on the station on Saturday for some time.

You have not noticed any perceptible difference? – No, he came down to see me at our place during the week, and he seemed very nice.

Inspector Thwaites stated that at about 20 minutes to 9 on Saturday night, the 29th April, he was called by the last witness, Mrs. Watson, to the house in Duke Street lately occupied by the deceased, John Harry Watson. His attention was then drawn to the washhouse door, which was fast on the inside. Witness burst the door open, and found deceased hanging by some webbing (produced). He immediately cut deceased down, and got the body outside into the yard. Witness pulled the clothing from the neck, and the body being warm, tried artificial respiration, but it was no use. In the meantime he called for someone to run for a doctor, and Dr. Huey arrived in a few minutes, and pronounced life to be extinct. The body was hanging about a foot from the floor. There was a step-ladder standing nearby from which deceased had apparently stepped. There was some clothing, apparently a shirt, wrapped around the beam about six-ply thick to keep the beam from cutting the webbing. Witness searched the body, and amongst other things, found a razor in one of the pockets. There was no document or anything to throw any light upon the affair.

The Coroner: There were no papers of any kind? – Nothing whatever, sir.

Did you notice anything else? – I found that the washhouse door had been locked from the inside, also there had been some grease put on the lock so that it would lift the bar up. The lock had not been used for some time and was rusted up.

Have you made enquiries to throw any light upon the affair? Yes, sir.

Have you anything definite? I have not been able to learn anything definitely. I saw him on the platform when the 11.48 train went out on Saturday, and he seemed quite in his usual way at that time. I have also learned that he took the milk in somewhere about 4 o'clock in the afternoon. I stood by his side for some time on the platform on Saturday morning, and he seemed as usual. He was accompanied by his wife and niece.

The Coroner said that was all the evidence he had to lay before them. There was no evidence, apparently, to be obtained as to the state of deceased's mind. His wife said he was very cheerful and bright that morning, and the Inspector said he was in his usual way. Mrs. Watson said he was worried about his work and about leaving Millom, and one thing and another, and had not been in very good health. That was all they had to go upon to show the state of deceased's mind. There was no evidence that his mind was unstrung, except they took that view of it. What was behind it all they had no means of knowing, and perhaps it hardly concerned them. Their duty was to find out how, when, and by what means the deceased came to his death. It would be helpful to them if they had some means of getting at the real state of his mind, if there was anything of such serious importance as might worry him and cause him to commit such a rash act, but the Inspector had told them that he had made enquiries and had been unable to find any definite information which would lead him to suppose there was some cause for deceased to hang himself. They would, he thought, have no difficulty in coming to a decision that deceased committed suicide, but as to the state of his mind, he (the Coroner) could not help them, and they must judge for themselves as to the state of deceased's mind.

Mr. Bradley said deceased had been in a declining state of health for some time, and was in a low way. He thought no one who was in his right mind would do such a thing.

Mr. Haynes: The reason given is that he was leaving Millom.

The Coroner: If Mr. Bradley had made that remark before a judge, I am afraid he would have had a rap over the knuckles for it.

Mr. Bradley: I think when a man does such a thing as that, he is not in his right mind.

The Coroner: I said it once, and got a very nice talking to from the Judge, but I got the man off, so I did not care.

The Foreman said the question was whether deceased was in his right mind when he did this, and he (the Foreman) was rather inclined to Mr. Bradley's view that a man hardly could be in his right mind when he committed self-destruction. His own view was that deceased died by hanging, and that he committed suicide by hanging, during a fit of temporary sanity.

The jury concurred in this view, and a verdict to that effect was returned.

FUNERAL OF THE LATE REV. J. H. WATSON

On Wednesday afternoon the remains of the late Rev. J. H. Watson were removed from Millom to St. Bees by the 11.48 train, and interred in the Priory Churchyard. Although very heavy rain was falling a number of St. Bees residents joined the cortege at the station. The coffin was covered with a large number of beautiful wreaths sent by relations and sympathising friends. The Rev. W. Hartley, curate in charge, and the Rev. R. S. G. Green, M.A., Millom, Conducted the service. Mr. Stafford, St. Bees, was the undertaker, and Messrs. Brownrigg supplied the cabs.

Several Millom friends journeyed by the same train to attend the funeral, including the Rev. R. S. G. Green (Vicar) and Mrs. Green, Messrs. J. Graham, J. Ormandy, A. Hutchinson, W. Watson, J. Hall, J. H. Davis, F. Davis, W. Dixon, R. A. Mitchell, etc. Deceased was at one time master at St. Bees Grammar School. The coffin was covered with wreaths, amongst others sent being those from:- His loving Wife, Parish Church Men's Bible Class, his loving Niece, Parish Church Sunday School Teachers, Parish Church Mother's Meeting, Parish Church Women's Bible Class, Parish Church Choir, Mr. and Mrs. Edward Tyacke and family

The Millom Gazette – Friday, May 11th 1911

MINISTERIAL

An Ordination service was held by the Lord Bishop of Carlisle in the chapel at Rose Castle, on Sunday, when, amongst others, the Rev. George William Lemmon, Literate, Curate of Holy Trinity, Millom, was admitted into Holy Orders as a Priest. The Rev. F. S. Vaughan was Gospeller, and the sermon was preached by the Rev. R. Mayall, M.A., vicar of St. Mary's, Windermere. The Ordinands were presented by the Bishop of Barrow-in-Furness and the Rev. H. A. P. Sawyer, M.A.

The Millom Gazette – Friday, June 7th 1912

1916

MILLOM VICAR'S APPOINTMENT

Just as we go to press, we learn that the Rev. R. S. G. Green, Vicar of Holy Trinity Church, Millom, has been offered by the Dean and Chapter of Carlisle, and accepted the living as Rector of Wetheral with Warwick, near Carlisle. Readers will learn this with many regrets, as the rev. gentleman is extremely well-liked and esteemed in the town and district. He came to Millom in 1907 from Croglin, in succession to the late Rev. W. Kewley. The announcement of his acceptance has, we understand, been published in the "Times" and "Manchester Guardian."

The Millom Gazette – Friday, May 5th 1916

THE NEW VICAR OF MILLOM

The Rev. R. D. Ellwood, B.A., rector of Torver, has been offered and has accepted the living of Holy Trinity Parish Church.

The rev. gentleman, who has for a long time been devoting the greater portion of each week by labouring as a munition worker at Messrs. Vickers Ltd., is well-known in the district, and the appointment should prove a very popular one.

On Sunday evening, the Rev. R. D. Ellwood announced to his parishioners in church the fact that he had been offered by the bishop, and had accepted, the living of Holy Trinity, Millom. The rev. gentleman succeeded to the office of Rector on the death of his father, the Rev. T. Ellwood, a few years ago, and previous to that he had held a curacy in Barrow.

The Rector has recently completed a twelve months' engagement at munition work at Barrow from where he visited his parish weekly and on just the Sunday services. He has taken ….t interest in the life of his parish, and, along with the Rev. F. T. Wilcox, Vicar of Coniston, he founded the Coniston and Torver Nursing Association three years ago, and which has been such a success. He represented the district on the Education Committee at Ulverston, and recently had the satisfaction of completing the efforts started long ago for the enlarging of Torver C.E. School, for which he acted as correspondent.

The Rev. R. D. Ellwood has also been closely associated with the "John Ruskin" Lodge of Oddfellows, which meets at Coniston, but ……… many members from Torver. He is a Past Grand of the Lodge, and one of its ……… The Rector's labours have been unobtrusive yet energetic and successful, and his parishioners will be sorry to lose one whose life has been so identified with theirs.

The Millom Gazette – Friday, August 11th 1916

ROMAN COIN FIND

Mr. James Coulton, of Holborn Hill, had an interesting find on Sunday. He went to look at the family grave in the Old Churchyard, when he noticed what he thought was a button lying near one end of it. Upon picking it up, he discovered it was an old Roman coin which had probably been turned up with the earth some time when a grave was being dug. The coin, which is a small copper one, shows signs of a human head and bust upon it, and also a Latin inscription, but both are at present almost illegible.

The Millom Gazette – Friday, August 11th 1916

INSTITUTION AND INDUCTION SERVICE
AT HOLY TRINITY CHURCH, MILLOM

A service of Institution and Induction of the Rev. R. D. Ellwood, B.A., to the Vicarage and Parish Church of Millom, and the Rev. Sherwen Sherwen to the Perpetual Curacy of Thwaites, was held on Wednesday afternoon at the Millom Parish Church. There was a large congregation present. The service was conducted by the Bishop of the Diocese; the Ven. Archdeacon Lafone, the Rural Dean, Rev. Canon Monnington, and the following clergy were also present: Rev. F. Pascoe (Vicar of St. George's, Millom), Rev. J. Harrison (Vicar of Whitbeck), the Rev. C. Wakefield (Vicar of Seathwaite), the Rev. W. S. Sherwen (Vicar of Thwaites), the Bishop's Chaplain, Rev. R. F. Diggle (son of the Bishop) and the Rev. G. W. Arnold (curate of St. George's). The churchwardens present were Mr. J. Singleton (Vicar's Warden) and Mr. T. Benn (Kirksanton).

The service commenced with the singing of hymn 209 A. & M., "Come, gracious Spirit, Heavenly Love," and the public institution, which is something of a novelty to church people, included prayers for the newly-instituted clergy, and the taking of oaths of allegiance on their part to the King and obedience to the Bishop of Carlisle, after which the ceremony of institution was performed by the Bishop.

The induction service, which is more familiar to Millom church people, was then proceeded with. The Archdeacon, taking the Mandate of induction, proceeded with the Bishop, the churchwardens and the newly-instituted incumbent to the church door, and laying the hand of the incumbent upon the handle of the door, said to him, "By virtue of this Mandate, I do induct you into the real, actual, and corporeal possession of this church, with all the rights, profits and appurtenances thereto belonging," adding, "The Lord preserve thy going out and thy coming in from time forth for evermore." The newly-inducted incumbent then tolled the bell to signify to the parishioners his taking possession. The duties of the incumbents were then set forth by the Bishop, to which they subscribed their assent, and prayers were offered for the success of their work.

The Millom Gazette – Friday, September 22nd 1916

1917

INTERESTING FIND AT MILLOM

A "find" of antiquarian interest was made by the Rev. R. D. Ellwood, Vicar of Millom, whilst digging in his garden at the Vicarage on Monday, when the rev. Gentleman unearthed a flint scraper which probably belonged to the Neolithic age. Implements of this description have been found in connection with pre-historic burial places, and near the spot where this scraper was found are the remains of a bloomery – a place where iron ore was smelted in the early days. There may or may not be some connection between the flint implement and the presence of the bloomary, and the coincidence is at least interesting. The date of the bloomery is very uncertain. There are several bloomeries in High Furness generally, especially on the banks of Coniston Lake.

The Millom Gazette – Friday, April 27th 1917

MILLOM PARISH CHURCH

Millom Parish Church is dedicated to the Holy Trinity, and last Sunday being Trinity Sunday, the festival of the dedication was observed. Special hymns were sung, and in the evening the anthem "O, how amiable," was beautifully rendered by the choir.

At the morning service the Vicar in his sermon gave a short sketch of the history of the church so far as it is ascertainable.

Speaking of the architecture of the building, he said: It ought to be remembered that the time of greatest activity in church building in England was during and immediately after a time of war. The Crusades were being carried on in the eleventh and twelfth centuries, and it was at that time that Gothic architecture was introduced into England. The Crusades were undertaken for the purpose of rescuing Jerusalem from the hands of the Turk, or at any rate of gaining access to the Holy City for pilgrims. Those who engaged in the Crusades gained new ideas from their experience of Eastern cities, and so the plain Norman style of architecture gave place to the pointed and ornamental Gothic style.

In their parish church they had in the chancel two small windows which had been considered to be Saxon; the North doorway was Norman, and the middle arches separating the middle and South aisles were early Gothic, whilst the tracery in the windows of the South aisle was late Gothic. The chief architectural beauty of the church has been the three windows on the south side; two of these were now blocked up, and it would be a splendid advantage to the church if some day they could be restored. The effigies in the east end of the south aisle were probably those of Sir John Huddleston and his wife Joan; he died in 1494. The fish window in the west gable belongs also to this period. It was formerly blocked up when there was a gallery at the west end of the church, but was opened out in 1862.

An indirect reference to the dedication of the church is found in the fact that in the year 1250 Millom had a charter for holding a weekly market on Wednesdays, and a fair for three days at the festival of the Holy Trinity.

Continuing, the Vicar said: I do not know how anyone can come to a church like this and worship without feeling inspired by the remembrance of the past history of the place; thousands of men and women who have lived and died for faith and freedom have hallowed these walls by their devotions. We owe gratitude to them, and to some in our own day who have helped to make this place a place fitting for the worship of Almighty God, and we in our turn are called upon to do what we can in this matter. We owe gratitude to our choir, to our Sunday School teachers, to all who help us to a deeper sense of the unseen world; and above all, we owe gratitude to Almighty God for giving us the power to apprehend the mystery of Divine truth, and to join in the worship of the Blessed Trinity. May he give us grace so to anticipate the transfiguring Majesty of His Divine Presence that we are at length made fit to worship Him face to face in Heaven.

In the afternoon a service of catechising for children was held, the intention being to revive as far as possible the old custom of a "Catechism Sunday." Despite the heavy rain, a good number of children and their parents attended, and the Sunday School teachers and choir were also present. The catechising was conducted by the Vicar, and the children's answers gave evidence of the careful training they receive in Sunday School.

In the evening the preacher was the Rev. C. Postlethwaite, Vicar and Rural Dean of Dalton, who delivered an inspiring and helpful sermon on the subject of the power of Divine grace.

The Millom Gazette – Friday June 8th 1917

RENOVATION OF MILLOM PARISH CHURCH

A meeting was held in the Mission Room, Holborn Hill, on Wednesday night to consider the advisability of having a bazaar for the purpose of raising money towards the cost of renovating the Parish Church. The Rev. R. D. Ellwood, vicar, presided, and it was decided that a bazaar be held in August in the Vicarage grounds.

The Millom Gazette – Friday, June 8th 1917

INTERESTING DISCOVERY AT MILLOM PARISH CHURCH

An interesting discovery was made at Millom Parish Church on Monday. The walls of the chancel were being freed from plaster in order to effect some necessary repairs, and this disclosed an ancient piscina and a credence shelf, on the south side of the sanctuary.

The credence shelf is the place where the elements are placed ready for use in the sacrament of Holy Communion, and a piscina, it may be stated, is a small stone basin used in the Catholic Church service to receive the water after it has been used by the priest in washing the chalice, subsequent to the celebrating of mass. The piscina is supplied with a drain pipe to carry the water out of the church. The piscina has in this case a small rounded stone arch placed over, and is a very beautiful, though simple, example of early Norman work. There is another piscina in the church, near the altar tombs of the Huddlestons, which is probably of later date than the one now discovered, as it possesses an Aumbrey – that is, a ledge on which alms were placed.

The discovery is of considerable antiquarian interest, and helps throw light on the date of this part of the ancient Parish Church. The probable date assigned to the work is about the year 1200, though it is possible it may be earlier.

The Millom Gazette – Friday, July 6th 1917

HISTORY OF MILLOM PARISH CHURCH

The Rev. R. D. Ellwood, Vicar of Millom Parish Church, has published a most interesting little book dealing with the history of the church, which should appeal to local people. The history of Millom is closely associated with the Old Church and the families who held sway over the district in past times, and the author has therefore had a very wide field to cover. He opens with a brief review of Cumbrian history from earliest days until the times succeeding the Reformation. Then follows a description of the Church itself, and the various features of particular interest, including the Hudlestone Monuments, the Cross-base, Sundial, Mason's Marks in various parts of the building and the Pitch Pipes, The Font, and Communion Vessels form the subject matter of another chapter. A list of the Vicars, Curates and Parish Clerks is given, with such information as is available concerning the various holders of the incumbency, and there is a highly interesting note on the Advowson contributed by Rev. Dr. Wilson, Vicar of Dalston, Cumberland. Other chapters are devoted to the various wardens who have at various times held office in connection with the church, the parish registers, with copious extracts, and finally the chapels of Millom. The interest of the book is enhanced by illustrations which include exterior and interior views of the Church, the Hudleston Arms, Crest and Motto, the Millom Effigies, the Masons' Marks, the Pitch Pipes and the Millom Font.

We congratulate Mr. Ellwood upon his enterprise in placing this historical record within reach of the Millom public. It has long been felt by many that a history of this most interesting district should be available, and now that it has been provided we trust it will meet with the appreciations which it undoubtedly deserves. As would be seen from our advertising columns last week, the book is on sale at the popular price of 1/-.

The Millom Gazette – Friday, August 31st 1917

1918

TRAGEDY IN CLERGYMAN'S HOME
FORMER VICAR OF MILLOM'S SON SHOT DEAD

We deeply regret to state that heavy sorrow has fallen upon the home of the Rev. R. S. G. Green, M.A., and Mrs. Green, so well-known in Millom, where the rev. gentleman was the incumbent of Holy Trinity Parish until a year or two ago, when he became Rector of Wetheral, near Carlisle. Their son, Reginald Hugh Green, who was only 16 years of age, left home on Saturday, taking a gun with him, and saying he was going to have a look at a rabbit trap. As he did not return he was searched for, and on Sunday his body was found hanging to a barbed wire fence, his gun beside him, with the muzzle pointing towards the body.

The Millom Gazette – Friday, February 15th 1918

FORMER MILLOM VICAR THANKS OLD PARISHIONERS

The Rev. R. S. G. Green, M.A., of Wetheral, has written to his old parishioners at Holy Trinity, Millom, thanking them on behalf of Mrs. Green and himself for kind messages of sympathy sent them in their recent great sorrow on the sudden death by a shooting accident of their son, Hugh.

The Millom Gazette – Friday, March 1st 1918

WAR MEMORIAL ORGAN

In the "Millom Church Parish Magazine" the Vicar (the Rev. R. D. Ellwood, B.A.) says that it is suggested that a most fitting memorial for those parishioners who have fallen in the war would be a new organ for the Parish Church. It is estimated that the cost of this, together with restoration of parts of the building which are in urgent need of attention, especially the windows and roof, will be about £1,500. The sum ought not to be beyond the parishioners' power; what was raised now could be invested in War Bonds until the proper time.

The Millom Gazette - Friday, March 1st 1918

MEMORIAL ORGAN FOR PARISH CHURCH

The scheme for the provision of a new organ to serve as a memorial of the soldiers from the parish and congregation who have given their lives in the European War has now been definitely promoted in connection with the Millom Parish Church.

The whole plan includes, in addition to the provision of and organ, the needful restoration of certain parts of the church which have fallen into decay. The total cost is estimated at £1,600.

The names of those who have fallen will be inserted on panels in the front of the memorial Organ.

The Vicar (Rev. R. D. Ellwood) is appealing for gifts and promises of gifts towards the fund.

The Millom Gazette – Friday, July 12th 1918

OLD CHURCH TEA PARTY

The Sunday Schools connected with Holy Trinity Parish Church had their annual treat on Wednesday afternoon. About 260 children of both sexes lined up in Holborn Hill, and the procession of daintily attired children made an attractive show as, headed by the Holborn Hill Brass and Reed Band, under Mr. T. Walter, and with banners and flags flying, they marched to the Old Church, where a short notice was held, and an address given by the Vicar (the Rec. R. D. Ellwood, B.A.), who, with his sisters, Mrs. W. Wilson and Miss Ellwood, took an active interest in the superintendence of the children's enjoyment. In the course of his interesting address, the Vicar pointed to the texts which adorn the spaces on the walls between the Gothic arches in the church, and told the children that these texts were put there about the year 1683, at the time when English churches were being repaired and beautified after the damage inflicted on them in the time of the civil war between Puritans and Royalists. The Royalist spirit was very strong in Millom in those days; Ferdinando Huddleston of Millom Castle had nine sons, who were all officers in the army of King Charles I., so the fabric of Millom Church suffered much but little harm except the spoiling of the tracery in the windows. The lesson impressed on the children was that the reverent care of an ancient parish church is a solemn trust which has been handed on to us from the men who in days long gone by were ready to give their lives for such a cause.

The children were accompanied by the Sunday School superintendent, Mr. H. Jenkinson, and the following teachers: Messrs. F. Knipe, H. Cooper, R. Knowles and H. Munroe, Mrs. Cartwright and the Misses A. Fox, F. Scott, K. Wall, D. Tyson, M. Lewthwaite, Preston, G. Preston, D. Riley, M. Singleton, Robinson, E. Coward and A. Bell with Mr. W. J. Davis, choirmaster and secretary of the Men's Bible Classes, while Mr. Jacob Singleton attended to the business side of the affair.

Tea was partaken of in relays at the school, and the usual sports and games were indulged in in the adjacent field (kindly lent for the occasion by Mr. W. Sawrey Watson), where the band also played selections, and a pleasant and enjoyable time was spent.

The Millom Gazette – Friday, August 2nd 1918

1919

MEMORIAL ORGAN AND RENOVATION FUND

The Vicar and parishioners of Holy Trinity Parish have raised £1,171 so far for the memorial organ in memory of the fallen and the renovation fund in connection with the Old Parish Church

The Millom Gazette – Friday, April 11th 1919

EASTER VESTRIES

HOLY TRINITY, MILLOM

The Vicar of Millom (Rev. R. D. Ellwood, B.A.), presided at the Easter Vestry of Holy Trinity Parish Church on Monday night. There were also present: Messrs. J. Singleton (vicar's warden), W. S. Watson (people's warden), R. A. Mitchell, H. Jenkinson, T. Cranke, W. Wall, M. Tyson, W. K. Atkinson and J. Dixon (sidesmen).

The meeting opened with prayer, after which the Vicar presented the statement of accounts. In Holy Trinity parish there was a balance in hand last year of £24 13s. 2d.; receipts amounted to £189 2s. 2d., and there was a balance over expenditure at the end of the year of £29 15s. 9d., an increase over the preceding year. An account for the Mission Room was furnished by Mr. Jenkinson.

The balance sheet and statement of accounts were passed on the motion of Mr. Jenkinson.

The Vicar again proposed Mr. Jacob Singleton as his warden. Mr. Singleton had consented to act, and his knowledge of the parish had, said the Vicar, been most valuable and helpful.

Mr. Singleton said he was at all times pleased to do anything he could.

Mr. Cranke proposed, and Mr. Mitchell seconded, the re-election of Mr. W. S. Watson as people's warden, Mr Mitchell saying that they had all been very pleased with the way in which Mr. Watson had carried out his duties.

Mr. Watson, in accepting the office, said it was a pleasure to him to do anything he could for the church.

Coming to the election of sidesmen, the Vicar said they had hitherto all been appointed by the meeting. There was something to be said for the procedure in some other places, where some of the sidesmen were nominated by the Vicar. However, the system in vogue in that parish had worked well in the past, and he thought it would be best to continue it this year.

Mr. Singleton proposed that the whole of the present sidesmen be re-elected, with a hint that one or two of them might improve in the matter of attendances. Mr. Benn seconded, and it was carried. The list of the sidesmen is as follows:- Messrs. W. K. Atkinson, J. W. Brockbank, W. T. H. Cartwright, T. Cranke, J.

Dixon, H. Fearon, J. Graham. T. H. Hodgson, H. Jenkinson, D. Jordan, H. Kirby, R. A. Mitchell, G. H. Scott, H. Shaw, J. K. Shephard, M. Tyson and W. Wall.

THE VICAR'S ADDRESS

The Vicar next gave details of some of the church's activities. They had 320 children in the Parish Sunday School, and 60 more at The Hill and Kirksanton, and he paid tribute to the careful and devoted work of the superintendents and teachers. He desired to acknowledge also the work done for the church by the Men's, Women's and Girls' Bible Classes, and those in charge of them, and said that they hoped in the future to have a special class for young men. More than 100 of the men in the parish had been in the war, and many had, alas, been called upon to make the supreme sacrifice. He expressed his appreciation of the valuable services of the choir, and said that they had long hoped against hope that their organist, Mr. John Henry Davis, might return to them, but he had unfortunately fallen in the war, and they could only bow their heads in reverent submission to the Divine Will. Since then Mr. Hall had come from his retirement to assist them, and he (the Vicar) desired to thank him, also Miss K. Wall and Mr. W. J. Davis, who, as choirmaster, did such good work. Turning to the financial side, he said that the affairs of the church were in good condition. The congregations had been maintained in a happy spirit. With regard to the memorial organ and church renovation fund, they had raised over £1,100, and he wished to thank all the collectors who had helped in this result for their active work, especially Mr. John Graham. He (the Vicar) had been in communication with the Church Crafts League, and the Society for the Preservation of Ancient Monuments, and Mr. Forsyth (an authority on the subject) was coming soon for a consultation. The were most anxious that nothing should be done to destroy the ancient character of the church.

THE ANCIENT SUNDIAL

Mr. R. A. Mitchell introduced the subject of having a new sundial placed in the pillar then in the churchyard.

The Vicar said he had had this subject under consideration for some time; he went to the extent of getting out a suitable motto, and also obtained prices for dials from a firm. He had thought about bringing up the matter in connection with the forthcoming renovation of the church. The dial pillar in the churchyard was very ancient, probably dating from about 1460, and had on it the arms of Broughton Tower, from whence it had probably been removed in the early days.

Mr. Singleton was willing to present a new sundial, and eventually it was resolved, on the motion of Mr. Mitchell, that the meeting approved of the restoration of the ancient sundial, and sanctioned this work being done when the time came.

The Millom Gazette – Friday, April 25th 1919

A RELIC OF BYGONE DAYS

The old sundial in Holy Trinity Churchyard. Images © Bry Cooper

The old sundial in Holy Trinity Churchyard. Images © Bry Cooper

In resetting the sundial post in the Old Parish Churchyard, Millom, preparatory to fixing a new dial plate, it was discovered that the base had been set up on various pieces of sandstone building material, including, it is interesting to note, a piece of tracery belonging to one of the south windows. It is hoped this may eventually be replaced in the window when the forthcoming restoration is undertaken. It is commonly known that the original windows were defaced when Millom Castle was attacked by Cromwell's Puritans in 1644. The Castle was a Royalist stronghold at the time.

The Millom Gazette – Friday, May 16th 1919

PUBLIC NOTICES.

MILLOM PARISH CHURCH.

FESTIVAL OF THE DEDICATION

Trinity Sunday, June 15th.

SERVICES—Holy Communion 8 a.m., Morning Prayer 10-30 a.m., Children's Service 2 p.m., Evensong 6-30.

The New Sun Dial will be Dedicated after the Morning Service.

The Preacher Morning and Evening will be the Very Rev. The Dean of Carlisle.

The Millom Gazette – Friday, June 13th 1919

MILLOM'S ANCIENT SUN DIAL

DEDICATION SERVICE AT PARISH CHURCH

An object of considerable historical interest in the picturesque churchyard of the Millom Old Parish Church has been the ancient carved stone pillar upon which in earlier times there rested a sun dial. Owing to the private generosity of the Vicar and Churchwardens, a new brass dial plate was recently procured and place upon the stone pillar which stood as a relic of a by-gone age, so that once again there stands a complete sun dial in the churchyard. It was solemnly dedicated in due form last Sunday morning by the Dean of Carlisle (Dr. Hastings Rashdall) who was the special preacher for the day, which was the Festival of the Dedication of the Church, in the presence of a large number of parishioners.

After the morning service a procession was formed from the church to the garth on the southern side. It was led by the choir, headed by Mr. W. J. Davis (choirmaster), after which came the Dean of Carlisle, accompanied by the Vicar of Millom (Rev. R. D. Ellwood, B.A.), while the parishioners followed and stood in a circle around the dial, upon which the new plate shone brightly.

The Vicar said they had assembled there that morning to dedicate to the glory of God and the benefit of the parishioners their new sun dial. The ancient post formed a link between the days that were past and the days that were to come. The post had four sides, and on two of them were the coats of arms of the family of Hudleston, who formerly lived and ruled at Millom Castle, adjacent to their church. On one of the other sides of the post there were the arms of a family called Chaucer, and on the remaining side the Broughton family. The old sun dial carried them back to the time of the Crusades, when the knights and men-at-arms were fighting for the delivery of the Holy Land from the infidel, and particularly for the preservation of the Holy Sepulchre from the hands of the despoilers. The Crusaders were inspired by their faith in God to do mighty deeds for their fellow-men and for their religion. The sun dial would lead their thoughts to the sunlight which came from God, and which would influence them for good in their hearts and lives. It would be a link between their past and their future; it would remind them of the holy men who had lived about there in bygone days, and inspire their faith in the future.

The Dean then recited the following prayer of Dedication: "Almighty and Everlasting God, the Creator of all things, Who causest the earth to circle round the sun, and governest all things by Thy wisdom and Thy love, we dedicate this gift to Thee and to the service of Thy church, praying Thee that we may constantly remember the shortness of life and the preciousness of time, and may so use each fleeting hour in the service of Thee and our brethren as to fit us for that eternal life to which Thou art leading us through Thy Son. Amen."

The choir then sang the hymn "O God, our Help in Ages past," and the ceremony closed with the Benediction, pronounced by the Dean.

The new dial plate has on it an equation table showing how much the clock is before or after the dial time at different periods of the year. The inscription on the dial plate is: "Light with sunshine, Lord, the good; Shadow evil with Thy Rood." The rood being, of course, the ancient name for the Cross. On a small shield on the plate is the inscription: "Millom Parish Church, 1919."

The Millom Gazette – Friday, June 20th 1919

PARISH CHURCH WAR MEMORIAL

The subscription list to the memorial organ and church restoration fund in connection with Holy Trinity Parish Church, Millom, amounted on July 24th to £1,292 6s 10d.

The Millom Gazette – Friday, August 1st 1919

1920

LOUTH DISASTER RELIEF FUND

At Millom Parish Church on Sunday last, collection was given to the Louth Disaster Relief Fund. The Vicar, in the course of his morning sermon, alluded to the custom in bygone times of sending a "brief" to the parish churches in England for the relief of disaster. These briefs became so numerous in the 17th century that they became a great burden, and gradually fell into disuse. Pepys in his Diary complains "30 June, 1661 (Lord's Day) To church where we observe the trade of briefs is come now up to so constant a trade every Sunday that we resolve to give no more to them."

An appeal was made for help in the disaster at Louth, a quotation being made from the account of an eye-witness of the splendid way in which the town was bearing the calamity. The collection amounted to £5 6s. 9d.

The Millom Gazette – Friday, June 18th 1920

VESTRY MEETING

A vestry meeting was held in the Parish Church Vestry on Monday evening last. There was a good attendance, and the Vicar presided.

A design for a Memorial Tablet, prepared by Mr. A. A. Jones, was submitted, and a copy of the proposed inscription, and an estimate of cost.

After consideration and inspection of the proposed site for the tablet, it was agreed that application should be made to the Consistory Court at Carlisle on Sept. 14th next, for a faculty.

The faculty will include the moving of an existing tablet to the memory of the late Reverend Henry Pickthall to a more suitable place in the chancel near the memorial tablets to other Vicars, and the consequent enlargement of the space on the north wall of the aisle for the proposed War Memorial Tablet

The Millom Gazette – Friday, August 8th 1920

CUMBERLAND MEMORIALS
FACULTIES GRANTED BY CARLISLE CONSISTORY COURT

At Carlisle Consistory Court on Tuesday, Chancellor Campbell granted faculties for several war memorials.

The Vicar and churchwardens of Holy Trinity, Millom, were given authority to remove from the north wall of the nave of that church a memorial tablet to the Rev. Henry Pickthall and his wife, and to place it on the north wall of the chancel, and to place on the north wall of the nave a tablet of white marble in memory of the parish and congregation who gave their lives in the war.

Authority was given to the Vicar and churchwardens of St. Luke's, Haverigg, Millom to erect a stone cross in the churchyard in memory of the men of Haverigg who lost their lives in the war.

The Millom Gazette – Friday, September 17th 1920

PARISHIONERS GIFT TO MILLOM VICAR

The somewhat limited capacity of the Mission Room was taxed to its utmost on Monday evening last, on the occasion of a presentation to the Vicar, the Rev. R. D. Ellwood, who will shortly leave the neighbourhood in consequence of his acceptance of the offer of the benefice of Whittingham, Northumberland.

The meeting was presided over by Mr. J. Singleton (Vicar's warden), who extended thanks to subscribers who supported the scheme (which, when originally promoted, was to purchase a motor-car or cycle for the use of the Vicar). He knew their Vicar before he came to Millom – while he was Rector of Torver – and remembered having a letter from the Bishop in which the appointment of Mr. Ellwood was announced. Since coming to the parish, Mr. Ellwood had discharged all his duties in a perfectly able and amicable manner, and they were all exceedingly sorry to lose him. It was mainly through the endeavours of the Vicar that such a large amount of money had been raised for the church restoration scheme, and their best wishes went with him for his success in his new undertaking, and that he would receive equal support in his work from his new parishioners to that given him in Millom. The speaker then called upon Councillor W. D. Barratt to make the presentation.

Mr. Barratt excused himself from speechmaking on the plea that Mr. Ellwood would prefer to get the affair finished as quickly as possible, said he was sure he was voicing the feelings of everybody in the parish when he said how deeply they all regretted the rev. gentleman's departure. He had very great pleasure in asking the Vicar to accept the gift (an envelope containing notes to the value of £100) from the parishioners, with their best wishes for his welfare in his new sphere of activities - (applause).

In replying, the Vicar said he found the occasion rather too trying to express himself adequately in words; he remembered other similar occasions, but had never experienced such depths of kindly feeling as he did that evening. He felt it was on his conscience to say, however, that it appeared very much as though he has "started a hare," so to speak, in the church, but he felt definitely certain that the people in the parish in whose hands the affairs and alterations to the church were left were able to carry it out with the utmost respect and veneration for the work of the past and for the continuity of the church. He had had dreams of worshipping with them under new conditions, but they had been dispelled; he hoped that God would spare him to come at some future time and worship with them. He felt quite certain that the Ecclesiastical Authorities were convinced that the people of the parish, if things were left in their hands for a while, would continue to stick to their work, and carry things out quite as successfully as formerly. He had had great difficulty in making up his mind to go, but he had been used to country work, and that had greatly influenced him. He had, before he came to live in Millom, always enjoyed his visits to the town, had liked the people more whilst he had stayed amongst them and, if possible, even more now he was leaving. He remembered about eight years ago being at a club walk and dinner in Millom, and the success of "The Two Companies" was proposed. He did not know who they were, they might have been theatrical companies – (laughter) – but he had since found out that everything locally was bound up in the prosperity of the two companies. It had been good to observe the feeling of concord between employers and employed in this district, a feeling he had done his best to help, and he sincerely hoped the spirit of harmony and concord would continue to exist. The Vicar concluded with a further word of thanks, and expressed the hope that he be remembered by his parishioners, as he would remember them – (applause).

Mr. H. J. Kirby (sidesman), associating himself with the remarks made by Councillor Barratt, spoke of the true friendship which had been extended to them by their Vicar. He had been born and brought up in the neighbourhood, and, as a student of human nature, had, during his sojourn in Millom, handled the people in a manner in which friction had been successfully avoided. He hoped that in the future they would be provided with a vicar who could also handle the congregation with the same tact – (applause).

Mr. S. Watson (people's warden), supported, and added that during the four years Mr. Ellwood had spent with them no one had got on better with the Vicar than he had. They were exceedingly sorry to lose him, and Miss Ellwood, too, but hoped they would be as happy in their new parish as they had been in Millom – (applause).

Mr. G. H. Scott moved a vote of thanks to Councillor Barratt for making the presentation, and also expressed his regret at the impending departure of the Vicar. Councillor Barratt suitably acknowledged, and the meeting closed with prayer.

The Millom Gazette – Friday October 8th 1920

AN ENTERTAINMENT

Will be held in the

Co-op. Hall, Wednesday, Oct. 27th

Proceeds in aid of the Parish Church Restoration and Organ Fund.

The following Ladies and Gentlemen have kindly consented to take part:

The Hon. Miss D. Cross.
Miss F. Stevens (Cleator Moor).
  "   M. Towers.
Mr. W. E. Thompson.
 " W. J. Woodruff.
 " W. D. Barratt.

Part Songs by Millom Parish Church Male Voice Choir. (Conductor, Mr. W. J. Davis).

Humorous Sketch by Hon. D. Cross & Party.

Chair to be taken at **7-45** by the **Rev. R. D. ELLWOOD.**

PRICES OF ADMISSION: 3/- and 2/- (Reserved) and 1/-

Seats may be booked at Miss Nicholson's, Market Sq.

The Millom Gazette – Friday, October 22nd 1920

CONCERT AT MILLOM

The accommodation offered by the Co-operation Hall was on Wednesday evening taxed to its utmost on the occasion of a concert arranged in aid of the Millom Parish Church Restoration and Organ Fund. The Vicar, Rev. R. D. Ellwood, presided, and expresses his pleasure at the entertainment being patronized by so large an audience, and the fact that unforeseen circumstances did not in any way cause any curtailment of the programme. The opening item was a quartette contribution by the Hon. D. Cross, Miss M. Towers, Mr. W. E. Thompson and Mr. W. D. Barratt – a talented party whose contributions were vastly appreciated. Mr. J. Woodruff (baritone) was in excellent voice, and was encored on each occasion, similar demands being made upon Miss. F. Stevens, the famous cellosist of Cleator Moor and Mr. W. E. Thompson (tenor, of Barrow). The Hon. D. Cross also sang with such marked effect in her song, "Philomel," that here again an encore was the popular verdict. Miss M. Graham, at the piano, fulfilled the duties of accompanist in a highly efficient manner, displaying exquisite technique. The Millom Parish Church Male Voice Choir (conducted by Mr. W. J. Davis) were heard to decided advantage in the part song, "Comrades in Arms" and "Drake's Drum" (Mr. W. Griffin, F.I.G.C.M., F.V.C.M., accompanying the latter contribution).

The second portion of the entertainment was a humourous sketch, "In the Cellar," – scenes in the cellar of 300 Grosvenor Square in November 1917, during an air raid. The characters had been judiciously allotted, viz.: Lord Kidderminster, Mr. W. I. Menzies; Lady Kidderminster, Hon. D. Cross; Stella (their daughter), Mrs. A. A. Jones; Lieut. Hugh Ashford, Mr. A. A. Jones; Florrie (a maid), Mrs. R. Fawcitt; Albert (Master Eric Davis). The humour of the piece was well maintained throughout, and the abilities of the participants were evidently highly appreciated. The evening's programme concluded with the singing of the National Anthem.

Mrs. W. D. Barratt, as organiser, deserves every commendation on the arrangement and success of the effort.

The Millom Gazette – Friday October 29th 1920

MISHAP TO FURNITURE VAN

The Rev. R. D. Ellwood, late Vicar of Millom, commenced duty in his new parish of Whittingham, Northumberland, on Sunday last. The furniture belonging to the rev. gentleman was removed by road on Saturday in a motor-van belonging to a Penrith firm, and whilst negotiating a steep decline on Gawthwaite Moor the van skidded, collided with a stone wall, overturned and was partially wrecked. The furniture was strewn for a considerable distance along the road, and several pieces were badly damaged, especially sideboards and bookcases. Fortunately, the driver and his assistant escaped injury. Help was obtained from Ambleside and the debris cleared away. The remainder of the furniture is being sent by rail.

The Millom Gazette – Friday, November 19th 1920

1921

INSTITUTION AND INDUCTION OF REV. D. W. IRVING, M.A

AT MILLOM PARISH CHURCH

Despite the inclemency of the weather on Wednesday afternoon, the Millom (Holy Trinity) Parish Church was well-filled upon the occasion of the institution of the Rev. David Whiteley Irving, M.A., to the Vicarage of Millom (by the Rt. Rev. the Bishop of Barrow-in-Furness – Campbell West Watson, D.D.) and subsequent induction (by the Ven. Archdeacon H. P. M. Lafone, M.A.).

Following the accustomed rites upon such an occasion, the Bishop Suffragan addressed the congregation from the pulpit, and said he addressed them on behalf of the Bishop of the Diocese, and wished he had been able to be present to speak to them that afternoon. The difficulties in getting about this diocese were well-known, and the Bishop, who had gone to Kirkby Stephen, had asked him to come to Millom and institute Mr. Irving. No doubt he would be coming before too long to pay them a visit, being a patron of the parish. That was a very important day in the history of the parish, and the congregation he would meet Sunday after Sunday. The loyalty in the parish was well-known, and Mr. Irving would look forward to the upholding of the very high opinion he had formed of them, and they on their part to the opinion they had formed of him. "If much is expected of us it spurs us on." Thoughts could not help but turn to the former Vicar, Mr. Ellwood, and the speaker said he must plead guilty to having caused the rev. gentleman to fill the vacancy in the parish in Northumberland. The Bishop said he had been told the work in this parish had been telling on him very much, and over there he would, with the help of a curate, be less taxed. No man in the diocese had been more faithful than Mr. Ellwood, and they had sent in him a good man, one of the very best in this diocese. Mr. Irving did not come to them to take Mr. Ellwood's place – that was the last thing he would wish. Mr. Ellwood had made his place, and one of the congregation had said to him, "We have missed him, we do miss him, and we will miss him." The man whom they had now got as Vicar was not one who did not like the memory of a late vicar to remain. Sometimes people said, "Ah, but the late vicar – he was so good at visiting," they didn't add that he was so bad at preaching, or at something else. And of a new vicar they say, "We don't see too much of him," but they didn't say he was a good preacher, or that he looked after the young men. They must not expect to find the same virtues in every vicar, but they should make the most of what virtues he has. He thought people were sent together in these communities to supply many of the gifts in which vicars from time to time may be deficient. Mr. Irving came to them with a splendid record, and in Barrow the speaker knew what they thought of him. Only that morning he had received a copy of St. George's Magazine, and if they wished to see what it contained about him they should get a copy. He came at a critical time in the history of the church, when every organised thing was undergoing a very critical investigation. Unless the Church (organised religion) got together in one spirit, and let people see they loved one another, "one heart and one soul in service," they would say this institution has had its day. A clergyman was not a man who could do all the work and answer all demands. People did not come to church now as formerly, and more opinions were being formed from books and papers. In a big parish a clergyman did not have time to get at everybody, and work had to be done through the laity, who reached out into all corners of the parish. There had been too much in the past of going to church to get something – a good sermon or good music. Now they must give – their share of the prayer, worship, inspiration, sympathy and loyalty because they were members of an association which was doing something for Christ, something which was too big for them to accomplish, and so each one depended upon the other to help and inspire. Their Vicar, knowing what the spirit has been in the parish, would look forward to that kind of loyal love and support from them.

And one word upon an infinite matter. They were noted for the support they had given their vicars, but the word had more than one meaning. More than spiritual support was wanted, and the speaker said it meant taking in hand the question of the stipend of the living, and making it more worthy of the ancient parish of Millom. He wished the laity would not speak of the clerical income in hundreds of pounds, but would say "£4 a week for this man" – and compare their own case. This parish did not give very much more than that, and there was a big house to be kept up. They wanted a first-rate man – they had got him, and they ought to keep him. There were such things as entertaining and subscribing to be done, and the worry often wore a man (and his wife, if he were married) out. Before the war it was possible to do miracles in the way of housekeeping, but it certainly was not possible now. He asked them to take the matter seriously into consideration, and make the stipend consistent with the dignity and size of the parish; the spiritual side of the work in a parish may be affected by the material side.

In conclusion the Bishop said, "I wish you and him years of happy fellowship together – he as a man you can trust; and may God bless you each and grant you great joy and prosperity in this union cemented to-day."

After the service a number of the visiting ministerial gentlemen and others were entertained to tea in the Large Room at the Institute by certain ladies connected with the parish.

The Millom Gazette – April 15th 1921

HOLY TRINITY PAROCHIAL CHURCH COUNCIL

The Vicar (Rev. D. W. Irving, M.A.) presided last (Thursday) evening over a fairly large attendance at the annual meeting of the electors. The secretary of the Church Council, Mr. W. K. Atkinson, read the minutes of the previous meeting, which were proposed and seconded for acceptance by Messrs. W. S. Farren and W. J. Davis.

The Chairman said that the Council last year comprised representatives of the various church organizations in the parish. They were nominated by such organizations and elected by the meeting of the electors. It had not been possible this year to approach the organizations for nominations, and he would ask consent for the re-election of last year's representatives, except in cases where removals had occurred.

Mr. F. Davis moved and Mr. Jos. Coward seconded re-election of all the eligible representatives, en bloc, to which the meeting agreed.

ELECTOR'S HESITANCY

RESTORATION OF THE CHURCH OR AUGMENTATION OF THE LIVING

The Vicar said the next business for the meeting to decide upon was whether to proceed first with the Restoration of the Church or the augmentation of the living. Whilst the Bishop of Barrow was addressing the congregation at the Induction service he had spoken of the necessity of augmenting the living, and a number of people in the parish had wondered since whether something ought not to be done towards the augmentation of the living and leave the restoration of the church and memorial organ in abeyance for the time being. Were they to tackle the two schemes together, or, if singly, which one first was for the meeting to decide. He did not wish to bias them one way or the other. There were three reasons why they should continue the work in connection with the restoration of the church, viz.: (1) it was a good plan to do one thing at a time, and they had already set out to provide a new organ and restore the church; (2) the organ was to be a memorial to the men who fell at the front; and (3) there was the danger that a thing once begun and dropped would hang fire when taken up again. With regard to the augmentation of the living, they were all agreed that the living was inadequate. He did not feel that it was a personal matter for him – it was a big question, and important in the interest of the parish and the whole church. What the church ought to aim at was to provide an adequate living for the clergy, and thus relieve them of anxieties in this direction; hundreds of churches in the country were not getting the best from their clergy owing to the anxieties they were faced with in keeping themselves and families. Masters in public schools were now warning boys that they must not take Orders, because if they did they would not be able to live. Another very important aspect was that up to the present time quite a large proportion of the clergy had been recruited from the sons of clergy, those who had been able to afford to send their sons to a University, but there are now very few who could afford to do so, and the Church was in danger of losing a large field from which to recruit. He felt, however, that the wisest plan would be to go ahead with the restoration of the church; he could get along quite well for a year or two, so that the augmentation of the living was not an immediate or pressing matter.

Mr. Jos. Coward asked if there was not a committee in existence to deal with the restoration of the church?

The Chairman replied in the affirmative, and said he understood that that committee had full powers, but since this other matter had been brought up they would appreciate a recommendation from the electors at that meeting.

Mr. H. J. Kirby said he quite agreed with the Vicar that they ought only to do one thing at a time. As Mr. Irving had expressed himself willing to go on as present, his opinion was that they ought to proceed with the restoration of the church. He fully recognised that adequate living should be given to the clergy. Some people were of the opinion that, times being abnormal, sufficient money could not be raised for church restoration, but probably by the time they actually put the work in hand things may be easier.

Mrs. Barratt enquired of the Chairman how much the funds in hand amounted to at present, and the Vicar intimated that they had about £1,300 or £1,400 in hand, but, judging from the reports, he did not think it would be wise to say how much more they would require – possibly another £1,000 at least, "not a great amount" – (laughter).

A voice: Say £2,000, Mr. Irving.

Mr. A. A. Jones said he understood that the augmentation of the living would mean an endowment, and that would be a big thing, and possibly hold up other schemes.

The Vicar said he did not know exactly what it would mean, but he would be sorry if it was only augmented by a small sum now and had to remain at that for about 500 years. If £400 was raised in the parish £400 would be granted from an outside source, and the living would be raised £40 or £50 a year.

Miss Watson asked in what position his successor would be if Mr. Irving should not remain in Millom very long.

The Vicar: He would suffer for my sins.

Miss Watson: But if you gave us your guarantee to stay, we could go ahead with the restoration and then consider the augmentation of the living.

Mr. J. Singleton suggested that they could start the augmentation scheme with a collection in the church.

Mr. W. J. Davis asked if it would be fair to subscribers to the Memorial Organ Fund to do away with the fund.

The Vicar: There has been no idea to take money away from that particular object for augmentation of the living.

Mr. W. S. Farren, as a member of the Restoration Committee, said he was in favour of going ahead with the scheme and consider means of raising money in the meantime. People had been asked to subscribe, but he thought better results might be gained from bazaars or in like manner.

The Vicar pointed out that this was a separate matter; even if the vicar was given £400 a year he could not provide a curate out of that.

A recommendation was passed by the meeting – put by Mr. H. J. Kirby and seconded by Mr. T. Wall – that the provision of a new organ and the restoration of the church be proceeded with as soon as possible, and the committee be asked to take steps to carry out the scheme.

Other matters briefly discussed were the Assistant Curate Fund and the Vicarage.

The meeting terminated with a few words of thanks to the electors from the Vicar for their attendance.

The Millom Gazette – Friday, April 29th 1921

WAR MEMORIAL SERVICE AT MILLOM PARISH CHURCH

Image from the archives of Millom Heritage & Arts Centre

On Sunday afternoon last, the War Memorial Tablet which had been placed in the church some time ago, was unveiled and dedicated at a special service, the attendance at which was such that the accommodation in the interior of the edifice proved totally inadequate. Extra seating accommodation had been installed but even so many had to remain standing and a very considerable number could not gain admittance to the church and remained in the churchyard, where the firing party were marshalled. Seats inside the church were reserved for relatives of the fallen men in whose honour the tablet was dedicated. The Vicar, the Rev. D. W. Irving, M.A., had charge of the service, the other clergy present being the Rev. C. M. Chavasse, M.A., M.C., (Vicar of St. George's, Barrow in Furness), the Rev. G. W. Arnold, M.A., (Haverigg), and the

Rev. A. Williams (curate of St. James, Barrow). Lieut. Col. W. F. A. Wadham, D.L., 4th King's Own Royal Lancaster Regiment, who performed the unveiling ceremony, was accompanied by Col. Thompson. Major W. D. Barratt (2nd in command, of K.O.R.L. Regt.), Capt. Gilbert, M.C. (in charge of the firing party, from the 4th K.O.R.L. Regt.), Capt. Taylor, and Lieut. Hodgson.

The local detachment of the St. John Ambulance Brigade, under Supt. S. Ford, also attended.

The service opened with the singing of the hymn, "Let saints on earth in concert sing," followed by sentences and prayers by the Vicar and responses by the congregation, and the singing of the fifth Psalm. The Lesson, taken from Wisdom. III., 1-9, was read by the Rev. G. W. Arnold, and then followed

THE UNVEILING

Lieut. Colonel Wadham – accompanied to the Tablet by churchwardens J. Singleton and S. Watson – prior to the unveiling, which consisted of the pulling aside of the Union Jack, said he was pleased to have been asked to come to the service to unveil the Memorial to the Millom men who made the great sacrifice in the Great War: during that period and since he had had a warm place in his heart for Millom lads. They were good men, and they did their very utmost – no man could do more than lay down his life for others. They had done it for a just cause: "For King and Country," and he was proud to honour them and to take part in that service. Col. Wadham then with the following words unveiled the Tablet: "I unveil this Tablet in memory of the following men of this Parish of Millom who gave their lives for their country in the hour of her great need, and whose names it bears" : James H. Allen, Edward Atkinson, George Coward, Thomas J. Brocklebank, Frederick J. Burn, John Carter, Samuel Carter, Casson Chadwick, Edwin Chadwick, Thomas Chambers, William Cornthwaite, J. E. P. Coward, John V. Cranke, John H. Davis, John Dawson, Robert Dawson, George Durham, John G. Eccles, Thomas C. Eccles, William J. Fallows, Andrew Fox, Stanley E. Hall, William Holmes, William J. Huddleston, William H. Jackson, H. Walker Jackson, Alfred Kemsley, Harry Kendall, W. Christopher Kewley, William J. Mackereth, William Martindale, William H. Milton, Joseph J Moore, Edmund Needham, J. Bewley Newton, James E. Parker, Herbert Pixton, Hartley Richardson, Thomas Raven, Samuel Redhead, Tom Robinson, Thomas E. Shaw, William Storey, Charles W. J. Thomas, Bernard J. Tyson, Leslie Tyson, Thomas H. Tyson, J. Arthur Turner.

A laurel wreath was placed in reverent homage under the memorial by Pte. Wilson Stable, a member of the original Expeditionary Force. The firing party outside the church then loaded and fired three volleys, and to the sounding of the Last Post on the bugle the proceedings became intensely impressive.

Of white marble, on grey stone, the Tablet bears the Huddlestone coat of arms at the top, the names of the 48 fallen, and underneath the following verse:

> "They shall not grow old as we that are left grow old,
>
> Age shall not weary them, nor the years condemn,
>
> At the going down of the sun and in the morning
>
> We will remember them."

The congregation remained standing while the Vicar dedicated the Tablet, but were asked to be seated during the singing of the anthem, "What are these?" (Stainer), which the choir rendered with great feeling, Mr. J. Thomas accompanying at the organ. Prayers were then offered by the Vicar, after which the congregation joined in the singing of the hymn, "Praise, my soul, the King of Heaven."

The Rev. M. C. Chavasse based his eloquent and comforting address upon the 41st verse of the 19th chapter of St. John's Gospel: "Now in the place where he was crucified there was a garden." In the course of his remarks, reference to the devastated garden overseas, the rev. gentleman said it had been a wonderful experience to witness the effect of Spring; old trenches were overgrown with new life, and the surface of the ground garlanded with poppies, and as one crouched under shell-fire it was thrilling to hear nightingales singing almost in No Man's Land itself, and as night crept on frogs croaked at almost every pond. It was life amid death – life springing from death, which death could not destroy. Was not the same contrast once more with them that afternoon? For so many of them the service meant a funeral service, it would be the only service they would have to mourn one they loved; he knew the agony it must have been to hear their name read out. This time of sadness tells of cups which cannot be filled, and brings memories of love and happiness of the past. And yet the uppermost feelings in their minds that afternoon were of happiness, joy and faithfulness, and they would not have it otherwise. Therefore as they had honoured the names of these brave men at that service and listened to the notes of the Last Post, and the sound of the volley – it may have been coming from miles away, over a soldier's grave in France – they should let that service transport them so that they might stand by the grave of the one they loved. There were three lessons it would teach: Life amidst death; hope; and hope springing from death. The war had been the tragedy of the world; the biggest blow of the history of the ages; God did not ordain it, He over-ruled it. In its moral aspects the war was a grim tragedy, it was so unspeakable that men thought of it as a war against war. They were the most terrible five years our globe has ever experienced, and yet no five years had ever produced more examples of utter selflessness and sacrifice for others. These men had suffered a crucifixion. The war gave a chance to millions of men living unnoticed lives, and they took their chance to show what they were made of, and they had made good. He would venture to say that no mother would grudge her boy that afternoon, and his brothers and sisters would not wish him back again for the part he played in the world was greater than anything they would ever do. One could only mourn the waste of lives, cut short in their promise of splendour, the cup of life held to their lips only to be dashed away after the first taste. Though nothing could ever fill the void in a life which had suffered bereavement, it was altogether un-Christian to lament life given in sacrifice. As regards this life, the sacrifice by these men during the war encouraged their comrades; in our own day they roused us, their countrymen, to realise that England must be made worthy of her martyrs. In the future they would inspire our children and our children's children who would come to that place of worship Sunday by Sunday, and who would learn these names by heart. By their early death these men had accomplished more than would have been accomplished in a century of ordinary life. Self-surrender, devotion and sacrifice had made them ready for promotion over that which we call Death, but which would be the life of real achievement; this is only the training ground for life eternal. They were far more ready to carry out the behests of God, by their early death, than if they had lived to a good old age in the ordinary way.

And in the last place he would have them remember the message of inspiration from the soldier's graves with the spring flowers upon them, the message of life conquering over death – Spring always speaks to us of the triumph of right over wrong. He did not suppose there was a more desolate spot than on the Somme front, in the region of Beaumont Hamel in 1917, where there was not a yard of ground without a shell hole, and men and mules were drowned in the black and stinking quagmire; the very river had been turned out of its course; whole villages had been beaten down into their very cellars and covered up by rubble, until you might have passed them and never know. But return a few months later, in late May or early June, and the ground was covered with a thick carpet of green and a variety of flowers; never were colours more glorious. One felt a great resentment against God – didn't He care? How could Nature proceed on her way so outrageously when the blood of men had been poured out like water? At length we understood: the triumph of right over wrong. Men could never destroy God, they could not alter or even abate one tittle of His morals, they were powerless to prevent the final triumph of God. The powers of hell had done their work. These men had died and we had won the war. Then lift up your hearts and shoulder your crosses, look on the fields, for they are green with Spring, and know beyond all doubt that if we play our part our redemption draweth nigh. The men had flaunted death, had made the sacrifice, and it was our part to face this life as fearlessly.

A collection was taken during the singing of the hymn "O Valiant Hearts," and the pronouncement of the Blessing was followed by the sounding of the "Reveille" by the bugler and the subsequent singing of the National Anthem.

The Millom Gazette – Friday, June 3rd 1921

MILLOM PARISH CHURCH GARDEN FETE

Through the kindness of Mr. and Mrs. C. Coade, a Garden Fete was held yesterday in the grounds of Millom Vicarage, in aid of the Parish Church Restoration Fund, the function unfortunately having to be postponed the day previous owing to the extremely wet weather, causing keen disappointment to all concerned, especially to Mr. and Mrs. Coade, who had made very extensive preparations for the event. Again on Thursday morning it seemed evident that the weather would once more prevent the affair taking place, but the afternoon was fine, and goodly numbers availed themselves of the opportunity of attending, cars plying regularly from the Market Square. The opening ceremony was performed by Mrs. Irving of Hawkshead, and the various stalls and side shows were well patronised. Mrs. C. Coade superintended at the Fancy Stall and Miss Watson ay the American Sale, whilst the Men's Bible Class Produce Stall also did brisk trade. Members of the Women's Bible Class attended to the wants of the company at tea. The inability of Miss K. Spedding to attend and give exhibition dances was regretted, but plenty of enjoyment was afforded by the 4th King's Own (R.L.) Band, which was in attendance by permission of Major W. D. Barratt). The Baby Show etc., and Miss M. Walker (palmist) were largely patronised, and at a concert, songs were given by Miss Barlow, Mr. W. J. Davis, Miss Fawcett contributing fancy dances. The public dance had again to be postponed, on account of rain, and will probably take place one evening next week, weather permitting. The winners of the Baby Show were:- 1st, (divided) Alfred and Fredk. Richards, twins; 2nd, A. Chadwick. Senior Nurse Barlow, superintendent of the Infant Welfare, Barrow, acted as judge. In spite of the unfavourable weather conditions, it is hoped that the financial result of the affair will be very good indeed.

The Millom Gazette – Friday, September 2nd 1921

PARISH CHURCH GARDEN PARTY

The recent Garden Party held in the Vicarage Grounds of Millom Parish Church realised almost £100, and the Restoration Fund will benefit substantially as a result.

The Millom Gazette - Friday, September 16th 1921

1922

THE PARISH CHURCH RESTORATION SCHEME

Writing upon this subject in the Parish Church Magazine, the Vicar says:-

"It must be generally known now that the question which the committee is trying to decide whether we ought to widen the chancel slightly by setting back the south wall, and build an organ chamber at the east end of the Huddleston Chapel, and have the choir at the east end of the church or keep the organ and choir at the west end, which might mean extending the west wall of the church, or at least of the Nave. We will want to know the feeling of the congregation at our next meeting on this question, so it will be good if it is generally discussed in the parish. I have no doubt that either scheme carried out under a sound architect would be a great improvement, but, as I have said, before we are committed with a heavy responsibility in dealing with the restoration of the church, and we must not hurry to any decision which has not had full consideration.

We would all, no doubt, like to push on the Restoration Scheme, and in many ways we must regret that we have not been able to move more rapidly, but we can remember that time, which may appear on the one hand to have been lost, will mean on the other, owing to falling prices, a saving of hundreds of pounds."

The Millom Gazette – May 5th 1922

ITEMS OF INTEREST

The Vicar of Millom, the Rev. D. W. Irving, M.A., in the current issue of the Parish Church Magazine, gives an interesting summary of decisions arrived at at a recent meeting of the General Restoration Committee, at which Mr. G. Gordon Stanham, architect, was present. The decision of the Executive Committee to extend the church to the west was confirmed, and it was also further decided to: (1) replace the windows on the north side of the nave by windows more in keeping with the general style of architecture in the church; (2) to restore the chancel arch in its present position, to raise the chancel roof, and set back part of the south wall of the chancel; (3) to replace the east window of the Huddleston chapel by a smaller one; (4) to restore the south door and porch. The floor will be lowered, and the south windows of the Huddleston chapel restored as previously determined.

The Millom Gazette – Friday, August 4th 1922

COMING EVENTS.

Grand Sale of Work in aid of **Millom Parish Church Restoration Fund** - - Wednesday, 16th August
To be held in Mr. Watson's Field, Millom Castle.

The Millom Gazette – Friday, August 4th 1922

SUCCESSFUL SALE OF WORK AT MILLOM CASTLE

During Wednesday afternoon crowds were to be seen proceeding in the direction of Millom Castle and Parish Church, attracted there by the Sale of Work which had been announced for that day. Owing to the sale being held the open in a field adjoining the school, and the weather being not too unfavourable, the afternoon's proceedings were more enjoyable than if the sale of work had been arranged to be held in some public hall.

Besides the large marquee in which the sale was held, and a similar one for concerts, there were several other tents in the field. In one of them Madame Linda did a good trade in delineating persons' character by palmistry.

The success achieved by the Parish Church Restoration Committee with their effort on Wednesday afternoon, fully justified them in holding the event, notwithstanding what might have been said respecting the volume of unemployment, and consequent reduction in attendance. Wednesday's function, however, gave no indication of this, as at the opening ceremony all the available space in the largest marquee was crowded. Everyone interested in the proceedings must have spent an anxious time on Wednesday morning, wondering if the torrential rain would abate in time to enable the sale to be opened. The weather conditions improved before mid-day, and no rain was experienced during the afternoon. Not until the dancers had settled down for a few hours enjoyment did the rain come on. However, by that time the committee had received all the available cash, so that financially everything was all that should be desired.

The Vicar, the Rev. D. W. Irving, presided at the opening ceremony, and was supported by Mrs. Morris-Eyton, the Rural Dean, Rev. J. Park (Gosforth), Canon Irving (Hawkshead), Mr. H. J. Kirby, J.P. AND Mr. Stanham (London). Amongst those present were: Mr. W. Lewthwaite, J.P., (Broadgate), Rev. Mr. Gardner, Mr. F. J. Mills, J.P., Mr. Coad, Mr. W. S. Watson, besides the resident farmers, &c.

The Vicar in his opening remarks said it had been remarked that brevity was the soul of wit. Though he could not be witty, he would be as brief as possible. It was almost 30 years ago since the late Canon Irving, who would always be revered in that parish, saw the need of restoring the Parish Church. This work of restoration had been in the minds of the people in the district all that time, and how they were endeavouring to be in a position to do the work. The object of the sale of work was to raise a fund for the restoration of the church. That would need a big push, and he hoped they would accomplish it. He could not tell them the actual position of the fund, or exactly what would be required. He thought they had £2,000, and it would need at least double that amount before they could really begin the work. However, he believed if they made a great effort, in the end it would be found quite possible to raise that sum. His chief business that afternoon was to thank all those who had given their time, their efforts and their money to prepare the sale of work they were holding that afternoon. It was quite impossible to mention everyone by name. He desired to thank the Bazaar and General Committee, the secretary, the treasurer, the pierotte troupe, the peoples' churchwarden, who had kindly lent the field at no small cost to himself. He was very grateful, too, for so many visitors coming that afternoon, and to them he extended a hearty welcome, and hoped they would have an enjoyable time, and that they would go away happy with the idea that they had helped to restore a church which was not only a place of worship but was one of the treasures of this old diocese of Carlisle. He had one further pleasant duty to perform, to ask Mrs. Morris-Eyton to declare the sale of work open. Knowing in Millom how much they owed to Broadgate, their committee felt sure that if Mrs. Morris Eyton accepted their invitation, the sale of work would be a success. He then called upon Mrs. Eyton to declare the sale of work open.

Mrs. Eyton said: Mr. Irving, ladies and gentlemen, it is a great pleasure to be here this afternoon. It was very kind of Mr. Irving to say such nice things, but she assured them that she considered it a great honour to be invited. It was always delightful to come back to their old friends who were born under the shadow of Black Combe, and those who lived at its feet. They knew that their object that day was a big one, to raise funds for the restoration of their beautiful old church. The people who built the church did so that it could be held in trust for the people who followed them. There were only portions of their ancient building that could still be preserved, but the restoration of their old church would be in accordance with the original plans which were made ages ago. The last two years had been sad ones for Millom, but after generations would be proud of them when they knew that in these hard times they did not neglect their church. In declaring the sale of work open, she desired that the result would exceed the expectations of the most sanguine of their committee.

Mr. H. J. Kirby, vice-chairman of the Parochial Council, proposed a hearty vote of thanks to Mrs. Morris-Eyton for kindly opening the sale of work. Though now living far away, like the members of the Broadgate family, she was anxious to do her best for the district, and he hoped that she would have a long life to continue her good work. She was always sure of a hearty welcome when she came amongst them. He desired to present Mrs. Morris-Eyton with a souvenir made by one whose work was always appreciated at Broadgate.

The Rev. J. Park, Rural Dean (Gosforth), said it was a great pleasure for him to come and help in this work. Church work was a work that not only required the help of the people of the parish to which the church belongs, but also the help of outsiders. They wanted to get out of the parochialism and to try and help one another. He was proud to state that most of the churches of the Deanery had been well restored during the last 40 or 50 years. Millom Old Church was a church that they were all proud of. It was a church of distinction throughout the district, but it would look very much better when it was properly restored. It might perhaps be a difficult matter to associate their views with the architect's plans of the alterations, but when they were done he was sure that they would give entire satisfaction. He sincerely hoped that afternoon that there would be a good response. He felt sure that the large number of people present would raise the necessary funds for the restoration of the church.. It was very enterprising for the people of Millom to attempt a sale of work when trade was so bad in the town. It was for the people, however, to put their shoulder to the wheel and pull together, and he felt sure that they would accomplish what they desired. From the number of people he saw before him that day, he felt sure that they were going to have a grand success.

Mr. Stanham (London), architect for the restoration, was then called on to say a few words. He remarked that he had taken a great interest in the work they were contemplating. To his mind there was nothing nobler than trying to rebuild or restore a house for the worship of God. They had in Millom a real gem. From an architect's point of view, it was splendid. Such a jewel of an ancient architect's and builders' work was not known throughout the breadth of the countryside, and it would be restored with as great a faithfulness and purity as the committee desired. The work had been entrusted to him, and it would be done with the one view that in the matter of restoration nothing modern would be introduced. They had to remember that their forefathers and the architects of old had such splendid ideas as to the construction of ecclesiastical buildings. He could assure them that it was the committee's wish that not a single object of interest would be lost sight of. Nothing would be removed in the course of the work that would not be restored to its original grandeur. They would he felt sure have no reason to regret having taken him into their confidence after they had realised what he hoped to be able to do. It was often said, does the work pay? He could only say that whatever money was spent would be returned one hundredfold. It was not 7 per cent. or 10 per cent., but one hundredfold. The money which they would be able to give that day to the committee would be expended with the greatest care. He therefore appealed to them to be as generous as possible in finding money for the restoration of their grand old church. He hoped when the result of the sale was known that their Vicar would be lifted up and encouraged in his work, and that he would feel what he had attempted to do was not attempted in vain.

The sale was then declared open, and business proceeded very briskly during the afternoon.

The committee are to be commended for their decorative skill in the arrangements of the stalls. A quantity of trellis work was procured and with this and fine sprays of Dorothy Perkins, Crimson Ramblers and other pretty roses. Every stall presented a very attractive appearance. The refreshment department was also so nicely adorned that few could resist the temptation to enjoy a cup of tea under such pleasing conditions. The Refreshment Committee were: Mrs. J. Wilson, Mrs. J. Dickinson, Mrs. G. Riley, Mrs. Jenkinson, Mrs Fender, Miss Atkinson, Miss Anderson, Miss Burns, Miss Preston, Mrs. A. Wall, Miss D. Cranke and Miss D. Tyson.

The stall-holders were:-

Cloak Room and Parcel Stall: Girl's Bible Class.

G.F.S. Stall: The Members, in the charge of Miss Bell.

Millom Castle Stall: Miss Watson, Miss E. Coward, Miss M. Gunson, Mrs. T. H. Hodgson, Miss Singleton, Mr. W. Kendall, Mr. T. Askew, Mr. T. Walker.

Congregational Stall: Mrs. Chappel, Mrs. Mrs. Coward, Mrs. Crossman, Mrs. Farren, Mrs. Howard, Mrs. Kendall, Mrs. Pixton, Miss Robson.

Plant Flower and Fruit Stall: Miss Mary Graham, Miss Fox and Miss Peggy Scott.

Women's Bible Class Stall: Miss Sykes, Mrs. Clark, Mrs. Johnston, Mrs. Lewthwaite, Miss Hodgson.

Candidates' Stall: Some very Industrious Little Girls in the charge of Miss Robinson.

Marsh House Stall: Mrs. Graham, Mrs. J. Bushby, Mrs. T. Bushby, Miss Johnson, Miss Wallwork.

The Vicarage Stall: Mrs. Coade, Mrs. Harrison, Mrs. Jones, Miss Monnington, Miss Wood and Miss Cowley.

Sweet Stall: Mrs. Davis and Miss Dawson.

Bran Tub: Miss Doris Kendall and Miss Ida Wilson.

There was also a shooting gallery in charge of Mr. A. F. Fox. An Aunt Sally, in charge of Mr. W. Mudge and Quoits, in charge of Mr. J. Pickthall. The "Ruins" Pierrot Troupe, consisting of Mrs. Barnes, Miss M. Graham, Mrs. Wilson, Master E. Davis, Mr. W. J. Davis, Mr. G. Park, Mr. J. Woodruff and Mr. T. Wall gave a series of entertainments in the tent allotted for that purpose. As the tent could accommodate about £5 worth of spectators and nearly half-a-dozen performances were given during the afternoon, this item on the afternoon programme helped materially to swell the proceeds. Miss K. Spedding's dances were also much appreciated.

The secretary, Mr. W. S. Farren, the treasurer, Mr. W. K. Atkinson and every other member of the committee were most assiduous in making the sale a thorough success. It is expected that when the whole of the proceeds are received a very substantial sum will be realised. At least one of the stalls took over £100.

The winner of the gold watch was not declared, as had been intended, owing to a number of the sheets not being received in time. The winner is to be duly announced later through the Press.

We are pleased to learn that as a result of the effort a sum of not less than £600 will be added to the Restoration Fund.

The Millom Gazette – Friday, August 18th 1922

MILLOM FACTS AND FANCIES

The other day a calculation was made of the population of one the most unlikely places, viz., a burial ground. The calculations went as far back as the registers gave any record, and it was found that if all those who had found their last resting place in Kirkby Churchyard could again rise up and assume their earthly forms, there would be to the number of 12,000. On this matter, it might be interesting to calculate how many departed beings have found their last home in the old churchyard at Millom Parish Church. Probably there are a greater number of those interred in early days whose remains have completely blended with the surrounding earth than those interred at a later date. Do the burials extend right way back to Saxon, or, rather Northmen's days? If so, the numbers must far away exceed Kirkby's record.

The Millom Gazette – September 8th 1922

1923

MILLOM PARISH CHURCH RESTORATION FUND

A SMALL

SALE OF WORK

(By Mrs. Graham and her working party). Consisting principally of Children's Warm Clothing, well-made, and of good materials, will take place in

THE DRILL HALL, MILLOM

ON

Tuesday, Feb. 13th. at 2-30 p.m.

Tea will be served at 4 o'clock, Music at intervals

ADMISSION (including tea), 1/- each

The Millom Gazette – Friday, February 9th 1923

MILLOM PARISH CHURCH RESTORATION FUND.

SALE OF WORK

At **MILLOM CASTLE,**

ON

WEDNESDAY, JUNE 13

To be Opened at 3 p.m. by The Hon. D. M. Cross.

STALLS, MORRIS DANCES, SONGS, BRASS BAND.

ADMISSION - 6d.

DANCE in Barn at 7-30 p.m.

The Millom Gazette – Friday, June 8th 1923

MILLOM PARISH CHURCH
G.F.S. SALE OF WORK
OPENED BY HON. D. M. CROSS

A sale of work in aid of Millom Parish Church Restoration Fund was held at Millom Castle on Wednesday afternoon, by kind consent of Mr. W. S. Watson. It had been originally intended to hold the sale in the open air, but the strong wind and a threat of rain persuaded the sponsors of the sale to remove indoors. Th sale itself was therefore held in the barn, and the teas were supplied in the schoolroom of the Parish Church. The effort was the work chiefly of the Girls Friendly Society candidates, directed by Miss Watson. There was a very satisfactory attendance at the opening ceremony, which was performed by the Hon. D. M. Cross, of Broughton.

RESTORATION FUND

The Rev. D. W. Irving, Vicar of Millom Parish Church, presided. He said they had hoped to be able to hold the sale in the ..ive of the Castle, but it had been so windy in the morning that it was felt it would be better to bring everything inside. He hoped they would not enjoy the sale of work any the less because of that.

The object of the sale of work was to raise funds for the restoration of the church. At the present time they had about £2,500 in the bank debited to the Restoration Fund. They had also about £250 definitely promised towards the fund, and that meant £2,750. They wanted, if possible, to have something like £3,500 in hand by the spring, and if they got that they would be able actually to start the restoration of the church. He hoped the sale would help them on towards the £800 immediately required.

He was very glad that Miss Cross was present to open the sale. Miss Cross was frequently asked to open sales, but they had specially wanted her to come that day because that sale of work was very largely the result of the Girl' Friendly Society, and, as they all knew, she was very interested in what the G. F. S. was doing.

In conclusion, the Vicar warmly thanked Miss Watson for what she had done to make that sale a success. He also thanked those who had helped so generously, and those who were present that afternoon.

A CREDITABLE START

The Hon. Miss Cross said she was very glad indeed to have come down that afternoon to open the sale of work. They all knew that the very large sum required for the restoration of the church could not be raised in one effort, and that repeated small efforts would have to go on for some time. It was very nice indeed to think that some of the juvenile members of Holy Trinity Parish had put their shoulders to the wheel and made a determined effort to help their church. She hoped it would not be their last effort by a very long way to help on the parish work. They were starting their career very creditably. The best thing those present could do second their effort was to make as complete a clearance of the things on the stalls as possible, and as far as their purse in these very bad times would permit.

The Vicar said they were very grateful to Mrs. Cross for her words, and he was sure the candidates would remember what she had said.

Miss Dorothy Black presented a raffia work basket to Hon. Miss Cross for her kindness in opening the sale.

MANY ENTERTAINMENTS

During the afternoon Mrs. Watson very kindly allowed the house and Castle to be open for inspection by visitors. In the evening an entertainment was given on the steps of the Castle by candidates of the G. F. S., some fifty in number. The programme was arranged by Miss Elsie Coward, and proved to be a most enjoyable one, including, as it did, action songs, solos, recitations, dances, etc. An exhibition of Morris dancing was given by G. F. S. candidates trained by Miss Sykes. Miss Gilchrist and the Rev. D. W. Irving rendered solos, and Mr. W. Thomas and the Vicar sang a duet. Miss Sykes officiated as accompanist, and for certain items Mr. Youart Harris played. Other items of interest were fortune reading and surprise drawing from the bran tub. The latter was in charge of Misses Doris Clark and Doris Kendall. During the course of the afternoon and evening Holborn Hill Band rendered selections.

THE TEA ROOM

Teas were served in the schoolroom, which had been tastefully decorated for the occasion. The tables were adorned by vases of lupins, paeonies, and Californian poppies, while the walls and ceilings were draped with green and white hangings interspersed with bunches of fern. The tearoom was under the efficient superintendence of Mrs. Coade, acting for the committee who had made the arrangements. Mrs. Coade had a host of willing helpers, including: Mrs. Scott, Mrs. Riley, Mrs. Gardner, Mrs. Alex. Wall, Mrs. Curry, Mrs. Ben Moore, Mrs. Jenkinson, Misses Burn, Ada Burn, Dolly Cranke, Winnie Cranke, Atkinson, Preston, D. Tyson and P. Mills. The following members of the Women's Bible Class also assisted: Mrs. Chambers, Mrs. Blamire, Mrs. Murray, Mrs. Tyson, Mrs. Higgin, Mrs. Woodend, Mrs. Cooper, Mrs. Johnson, and Mrs. Clark.

THE STALLS

There was a great variety of articles on the stalls of such quality that buyers were readily found. G. F. S. candidates had charge of the raffia and basket work stall and the fancy work stall, which were attended by Mrs. Pixton, Mrs. Robinson, and Misses Gunson, Singleton, Lewthwaite, Hogg, and Robinson. The cake and sweets stall was managed by Misses Graham, Short, and Peggy Scott. The congregational stall was under the charge of Mrs. W. Kendall, Mrs. J. Coward and Mrs. W. S. Farren.

It is estimated that the proceeds will be not less than £100.

The Millom Gazette – June 15th 1923

MILLOM PARISH CHURCH
A VENERABLE PILE OF SAXON ORIGIN
LESSONS IN STONE

A most interesting light was thrown on the probable origin and history of Millom Parish church on Sunday, when the Men's Bible Class was addressed by Mr. Gordon Stanham. The Vicar (Rev D. W. Irving), in his introductory remarks, paid a tribute to Mr. Stanham's ability as an architect, and stated that in view of the proposed restoration, he had taken a great deal of interest in Millom Parish Church.

ORIGIN IN NINTH CENTURY

Mr. Gordon Stanham said it was no light task to do justice to the lovable, venerable and splendid pile that was Millom Parish Church He ventured to think that there was not another such building with such splendid history as Millom Church had. The first question to be asked was "What is the age of the church?" After looking round he had been awestruck by the ancient stones which were in that building. He could not venture to tell them the age of each stone, but he could tell them what was his idea of their age. In his opinion the building was put up somewhere in the early years of the Ninth Century by the Saxons. There were several traces in the building of Saxon work. If they were to look around they would see stone upon stone showing age upon age. But there were stones there which denoted to those who had made a study of stones some work of the ancient fathers. It was, therefore, one of the venerable structures of the countryside. The next thought that was accrued was the shape. The original shape of that ancient building was almost a parallelogram. He intentionally said "almost" because the figure was not quite exact. One naturally wondered how and why that was. If they carried their minds back to what was known of the Ninth Century, they would know that in those days builders did not have steel tapes, they did not have even two-foot rules. They measured their land with strips of hide or hazel wood. He thought the Saxons had used strips of hide in this instance. Therefore they were not able to get the ground out with the delicacy of precision and exactness that could be attained to-day. Hide stretched, and the way a man held it or joined length to length varied. Therefore, they found that the south wall of the church as it originally stood was not of the same length as the north wall, the south wall being longer. The original part of the church was the nave, and the nave existed until the time came for elongation or enlargement. Doubtless the next step was the chancel. There was no record of this so far as he could trace, and he had searched the British Museum, the Office of Rolls, and other buildings in London, to find out what he could about their church. He had gone back to the time when he had unfortunately been unable to decipher the records, as these rolls were in Norman-French. Nevertheless, it was his opinion that the chancel had been added in the Eleventh Century. The next addition was the Hudlestone Chapel, which, in his opinion, was added in the Fourteenth Century. There they had the complete ground plan as they saw today.

THE WINDOWS AND DOORS

There were some traces in the church of Saxon windows. They might have seen the trace of one in the chancel, but there were other pieces of Saxon windows which he had found only the previous day. He had found one in the west end of the church, There were other pieces of masonry which denoted an ancient date of origin. There had been a doorway that was most likely north side, because they could read that in the north wall there was a circular headed doorway. The Saxons had not known anything but the circular form in masonry. The building had been, roughly speaking, rectangular, about 52 feet by some 30 feet in size, and doubtless had had a small number of circular headed windows and a circular headed doorway. These Saxon windows consisted of a narrow lintel with a circular head. They only let in a little light, but when the light got into the church it flooded the building. He thought they could draw a beautiful lesson from this, that once God's love found a way in it spread and suffused everything with light and love and beauty. The Early Saxons had never made their doors large, because God's house had been a sanctuary and not only a meeting place. These narrow doorways taught the lesson that we had all to go into God's sanctuary through the one door, but we had to go in singly. God's holy love led us up to the doorway, but we went in singly to the sanctuary, and, once inside we met a flood of love and light that made men of us.

THE WATCH TOWER

The speaker's survey now brought him to what he termed the time of the priesthood, when there was more ceremonial in religion. Their forefathers, he reminded them, were not taught by book, but by ceremonial and acts of devotion, they were taught through their senses. The priest required more room to perform the acts of devotion, and so the chancels were built. There were the remains of a priest's window in the northern wall of Millom Parish Church. The church, it had to be remembered, was a sanctuary, and that window was there so that the priest might always be watching and ready to give admittance. At that period the floor of God's house here had been about eighteen inches lower than the present floor, and there had been a doorway in the west end of the church, probably to admit the rush cart, for in those days there were no seats, but the people knelt on the rush-strewn floor.

They knew that the Hudlestone Chapel was erected in the Fourteenth Century by those who were in possession of the Castle at that time, and it was erected doubtless as a burial place for their warriors. In the course of his survey he had come across a very interesting sketch of the church, and on it there was depicted a tower, but whether it was at the west end, which was now the Hudlestone Chapel or whether it was at the other end he could not say. He himself believed that there had been a tower on the south-west corner before the Hudlestone Chapel was placed there. It had probably been built because the church was not only a sanctuary but a warning place, and the tower was used as a watch place, whence the people were warned of sudden danger. He could easily see how an army could gather on the hills around Millom and sweep down on the village. But a watch was kept on the tower, and the people were warned of the approach of danger. There was another lesson here because it was the duty of everyone to keep a watch for spiritual enemies. The roof here was not the original roof, and in his opinion there had been many roofs. The rest of the church was very modern.

STUDY STONES

He had given this brief sketch of the church, and now he hoped some of his ……. would make a closer study of the building themselves. He did not want them to take it all from him. He wanted them to go and see for themselves, and not only from the material but from the spiritual point of view. Ancients stones had lessons to teach and messages to give. When he had been there the previous day the stones had shouted out at him. He asked them to study stones and learn God's messages. Much of the power of a church was in its ancient stones. Their duty for the future was to re-stone the church in a material sense, and still more to re-stone it in the spiritual sense with the spirit of true and earnest worship of the Father.

The Millom Gazette – Friday, July 6th 1923

1924

MILLOM PARISH CHURCH RESTORATION
SCHEME APPROVED BY COUNCIL.
VICAR OUTLINES POSITION.

The question of the restoration of the Parish Church was brought before a meeting of the Parochial Church Council on Thursday last week. In laying the matter before the Council the Vicar (Rev. D. W. Irving) explained the present position. A scheme to restore the church and provide a memorial organ had been prepared by the Restoration Committee, but before anything further could be done it was necessary to have the approval of the Council. It was not for the Council to determine at that meeting what should be done, or, in other words, to devise a scheme, because that had already been done by a committee elected for the purpose by the parish. The Council were asked, however, to express their opinion on the scheme already in existence, plans of which would be presented to the meeting.

In submitting the plans to the Council, the Vicar said he would like to make clear what the considerations had been which had led the Restoration Committee to recommend the present scheme. The committee had been asked to make provision for a new organ and to restore the church, and it was not proposed to do more than this. The plans, however, would be seen to show an extension of the present south aisle or Hudleston Chapel to the east, and this had been felt to be a necessity for several reasons, but mainly in order to find more room. In fact, the committee had felt all along that the main problem was more room. Room was required first of all for the new organ and choir stalls. There was, the committee felt, no really satisfactory position for these in the present building. The church was already cramped, and to …. the new organ on the west wall of the nave, with the choir stalls underneath, as had been suggested, would only add to their difficulties and give the church a still more cramped appearance.

But more room was also required in the sanctuary and chancel, and to provide space for a baptistery (at present there was no baptistery), as well as for the more reverent and orderly conduct of the services. It was pointed out that that there was insufficient room at the present time for weddings and funerals. At a funeral the body had to be left at the back of the church, and they wanted, if possible when the restoration was carried out, to avoid the necessity for this.

Room at any rate had to be found somewhere, and the committee proposed the extension to the east as the most satisfactory solution of the difficulty. If this was done, then the organ would be given a position in the east end of the extension, and the choir stalls would be placed in a block next to it.

For the rest the plans showed nothing but what might quite accurately be described as pure restoration. It was hardly fair to say because alterations were being proposed that the church was being pulled to pieces. The committee all along had tried to make as little alteration as possible, but the fact was that in the past the church had already been pulled to pieces, and it was to their endeavour to restore it to its former beauty. It was accordingly proposed to re-open the windows on the south and the door which had been built up, and also to lower the floor to its original level.

As regards cost, the Vicar said the only estimate yet received was an approximate one of £5,700 - £5,000 for the work on the building and £700 for the organ. This figure, he said, might be found to be higher or lower than the actual one, but a point to be kept in mind was that the additional cost of the extension to the south aisle would only be £1300. The choice lay not between a larger scheme and a lesser one, but between a satisfactory scheme and an unsatisfactory one, and if the difference between the two was only £1300 it was nothing. He (the Vicar) therefore commended the plans to the Council for their approval, and hoped that the Council would not only pass a favourable solution on the proposals, but would also accord their thanks to the Restoration Committee and to their architect for the pains at which they had been in order to procure the best possible solution of the difficulties which confronted them in the work of restoration.

The plans were then laid before the Council, and there was a frank discussion on a number of points raised.

Mr. Jos. Coward said the main objection to the scheme was on account of the alterations proposed. There was not, and he had not found any objection in the parish on the score of cost, but people did not want the church pulled to pieces. The Vicar said that he thought a fair answer to that was that unfortunately the old church had already been pulled to pieces, and the committee were only trying to put it back as it was. Miss Watson said it would be altered, but very much beautified if the work was done. Mr. Jenkinson said the main thing was that we should all keep in good humour, as we had done that night, but he knew that some people were opposed to the scheme because the committee seemed to be using the money subscribed for more than it was given. The original idea was to put an organ in and restore the church.

The vicar said that what Mr. Jenkinson said was quite true, but the committee, after careful deliberation, had come to the conclusion that the organ could not well be put inside the present walls of the church, and so there was no alternative but to make room for it. The slight addition to the church proposed was simply to find adequate room for the organ; there was no idea of finding more seating.

Mr. Jones said he was afraid the parish would be saddled with a heavy debt, but Mr. Kirby pointed out that the committee had decided not to begin until 75 per cent. Of the money had been found, so that his objection had nothing in it.

Mr. Farren asked a question about the east end of the building. Why had not the extension been carried to the full length of the building?

The Vicar said that the sanctuary had been made to project in order to make it possible to keep the late Canon Irving's memorial window in its present position.

The following motion was subsequently proposed by Mr. Kirby and seconded by Mr. Cartwright:-

"That the scheme and plans recommended by the Restoration Committee be approved and the necessary formalities be proceeded with."

The following amendment was proposed by Mr. A. Jones and seconded by Mr. Jenkinson:

"That the new organ be lofted on the west wall of the nave, with the choir underneath as a preliminary measure."

On the amendment being put to the meeting, eight voted for it and sixteen voted for Mr. Kirby's original motion, which was therefore carried.

The Vicar said that the next step would be to make application to the Carlisle Diocesan Church Extension Society for a grant, and in due time application would be made for a faculty.

The amount which the committee have in hand now is over £3000, and other sums are promised. We are given to understand that any further subscriptions, either large or small, will be welcomed in order that the work may be begun at the earliest possible moment.

The Millom Gazette – Friday, January 25th 1924

MILLOM PARISH CHURCH.

PICTURESQUE

ORIENTAL BAZAAR

DRILL HALL,

Wednesday Next, July 2nd, 1924.

Opening by Mrs. HIBBERT at 2-45 p.m.

STALLS, MUSIC, WIRELESS.   DANCE AT 9.
ADMISSION - 6d.   :-:   TEA :-: 1/-.

The Millom Gazette - Friday, June 27th 1924

MILLOM PARISH CHURCH

As a result of the G.F.S. Bazaar held in the Drill Hall on July 2nd, it is thought that a sum of not less than £250 will be added to the Memorial Organ and Restoration Fund. We regret that in the account of the Bazaar the name of Mr. A. Wall, who was largely responsible for the actual building of the picturesque stall, was omitted.

The Millom Gazette – Friday, July 11th 1924

REBUILDING TOO DRASTIC

CHANCELLOR SENDS MILLOM CHURCH SCHEME BACK FOR MODIFICATION

An extensive for the alteration and restoration of Millom Parish Church came before Chancellor Campbell at a sitting of Carlisle Consistory Court yesterday.

The church is one of the most ancient in the diocese, and the drastic scheme of alterations suggested had aroused some considerable opposition.

The Chancellor, while admitting that the church needed a great deal of improvement and judicious restoration, thought it was undesirable that the church should be practically rebuilt.

He accordingly adjourned the matter for a less ambitious scheme to be prepared.

North Mail and Newcastle Daily Chronicle – Wednesday, July 23rd 1924

MILLOM VICAR GOES TO CARLISLE

The Rev. D. W. Irving, vicar of Holy Trinity, Millom, has been presented by the Bishop of Carlisle to the living of St. Stephen's, Carlisle. The Rev. D. W. Irving is a son of Canon Irving, of Hawkshead, and was formerly a curate in Barrow district and St. Stephen's, Carlisle. He is well known as a Rugby Union footballer, having played for Furness Rugby Union team and for Millom.

Lancashire Daily Post – Wednesday, August 27th 1924

MILLOM PARISH CHURCH

PETITION TO BISHOP OF CARLISLE

A meeting of parishioners of Holy Trinity Church, Millom, was held in the Mission Room on Monday evening for the purpose of considering a proposal for a testimonial to the Vicar (Rev. D. W. Irving, M.A.) on his leaving the parish for St. Stephen's, Carlisle. The meeting was fairly representative, and was conducted by the churchwardens Mr. G. H. Scott (Vicar's) and Mr. W. H. Watson (People's).

Mr. Scott, who was elected Chairman, said he believed he was expressing the opinion of the meeting when he said they were all heartily sorry that Mr. Irving was having to leave the Parish Church. They all knew the circumstances which had arisen, and he did not think the Vicar felt he wished to go. Certainly his people did not want him to go. Many of them had approached the churchwardens, and at a meeting of the wardens and sidesmen held about a week ago it was decided to call a meeting of the parishioners to discuss the matter of a testimonial.

Mr. Watson said that before they discussed a testimonial he would like to ask if there was any chance of the Vicar staying on.

The Chairman said that representations could be made to the Bishop and see what view he took of the matter.

Others spoke in favour of this course being taken, and ultimately Mr. Watson moved that a petition be sent to the Bishop pointing out that it was felt the best interests of the parish would be served by Mr. Irving remaining in Millom, and requesting the Bishop to reconsider his decision.

Mr. T. Bushby seconded, and the resolution was passed with complete unanimity.

It was decided to write direct to the Bishop, to notify the Vicar of what had been done, and to adjourn the present meeting for a week pending a reply to the petition.

The Millom Gazette – Friday, October 3rd 1924

REV. D. W. IRVING'S DEPARTURE

Millom is the poorer by the departure this week of the Rev. D. W. Irving, M.A., for the past three years Vicar of Millom Parish Church. He goes to Carlisle to take up the position of Vicar at St. Stephen's Church, and dearly though most of his parishioners would have loved him to stay in Millom, the old order must inevitably change, yielding place to new. The people of Millom wish him felicity in his new parish.

An earnest and conscientious preacher, the Rev. Irving has shown himself to be a worker and a real leader of the congregation. He knows the homes of his people, and has been a good friend to many. He has actively identified himself with every activity connected with the church, including the Sunday School, Bible Classes and Men's Institutes. He held an ideal of the church restored and made equal to modern requirements, but apparently this ideal is not to be realised meantime.

Mr. Irving preached at both services on Sunday. Both were well attended, the church being crowded at Evensong. At night he preached from the words "The God of hope give you joy and peace in believing." At the outset he said that Christianity was the only religion that contained an atom of hope for humanity and hereafter. He cited briefly other religions, and then went on to say that only in a Christian was there to be found an example of man as he ought to be. The savage was not man as God meant him to be, neither was the criminal, and even when looking at the emptiness of society one felt that all this mockery and vanity was not the life that God meant for man. At the close of his sermon Mr. Irving said: "I have been proud to be Vicar of this church for a period of three years, and I have been conscious of many blessings for which I am grateful. The best message I can leave you with now is "May the God of hope give you joy and peace in believing."

The Millom Gazette – Friday, October 24th 1924

PREFERMENT FOR THE VICAR OF SHAP

At the service at Shap Church on Sunday morning the Rev. P. A. Stewart, Vicar, said the Bishop had offered him the living of Holy Trinity, Millom, vacant by the preferment of the R. D. Irving to a Carlisle living, and he had decided to accept it, as he considered it his duty to follow the Bishop's lead. Millom had more than twice the population of Shap, but like Shap it was very scattered. He had spent five happy years at Shap, and it would be a big wrench to leave. The Bishop was anxious for him to change as soon as possible, and he hoped to go early in December.

The Penrith Observer – Tuesday, October 14th 1924

MILLOM PARISH CHURCH

We learn that the Rev. P. A. Stewart, Vicar of Shap, who will succeed the Rev. D. W. Irving as Vicar at Millom Parish Church, will not be able to take up his new duties this month. He will endeavour to come to Millom some time in December, and hopes to take over his new duties before Christmas.

SERVED IN THE RANKS

Rev. P. A. Stewart is an M.A. of Wadham College, Oxford. He was ordained Deacon in 1910, and in the following year was ordained Priest by the late Bishop of Carlisle. In 1910 he became curate at Kendal Parish Church, and remained there till 1914. When the war broke out he joined up as a private soldier, and served ten months in the ranks prior to going to France. At the end of that time he was appointed Chaplain, and later served in France, Mesopotamia and Palestine. In 1919 he returned to civil life, having won the Military Cross during his career as an Army Chaplain. On his demobilisation he was appointed Vicar of Shap, which position he will relinquish to become Vicar of Millom.

The Millom Gazette – Friday, November 7th 1924

PRESENTATION TO REV. D. W. IRVING

HANDSOME GIFT TO FORMER MILLOM VICAR

There was a very pleasant gathering in the Drill Hall, Holborn Hill, on Friday night last, when the Rev. D. W. Irving, M.A., Vicar of St. Stephen's, Carlisle, was the guest of his former parishioners of Millom.

Rev. Irving left Millom only recently to take up new duties at Carlisle, and the purpose of Friday's reunion was that might receive a gift in token of esteem and good wishes from parishioners of Millom Parish Church and other friends in the town. There was a splendid attendance of friends and well-wishers.

Several musical items preceded the presentation itself, but when the all-important moment arrived Mr. G. H. Scott, Vicar's Warden, who presided, said that really they did not want to have to give Mr. Irving a parting present. They would much rather he had stayed with them in Millom, but seeing they had perforce to make a present to him, they had done the best they could, and actions spoke more than words. Mr. Irving had been Vicar of Millom for just over three years, and during that time they had got to know him better, which meant to like him better. They believed, however, that he was going to a wider and fuller sphere of action, and a good deal of the hope and promise and success of life lay before him. They therefore wanted him to go forward feeling the friendship and encouragement of the Millom parishioners behind him, and to that end they had raised close upon £50 as a testimonial. They had bought something very solid for him, but it could be translated into something more tangible still, namely their appreciation of him and good feeling towards him.

Mrs. Scott, in a few well-chosen words, presented to Mr. Irving on behalf of the congregation of Millom Parish Church, a handsome silver tea and coffee service, and cheque.

REV. D. W. IRVING'S REPLY

Rev. Irving at the outset remarked on how much he had enjoyed the programme, and observed that there was no pleasure like listening to songs and seeing the singers in front of one. Continuing, he said sometimes it was difficult to speak because one had nothing to say, and sometimes it was difficult because one had so much than could be said. He felt that the latter was the case that night. He did not know what he'd done to deserve all this – the kind things that had been said, the beautiful tea and coffee service, the very handsome cheque and such a large friendly gathering that night. He would like to say something about the help Mr. Scott and Mr. Watson had been to him while he was in Millom. When Mr. J. Singleton had retired from the office of Vicar's Warden he had felt that out of all the good men there were for the position there could be nobody better than Mr. Scott. He now to thank Mr. Scott for all his loyalty to the Old Church and to its Vicar. He had also to thank Mr. W. S. Watson, the People's Warden. All who knew the church knew what the Watson family of Millom Castle had done for it. The Castle had stood there for centuries, guarding the precincts of the church, and for a long time the Watson family had done all they could to further the Church's interests. He was not sure they all realised what a deep interest Sawrey Watson himself took in it, no less than Mrs. Watson and Miss Watson. While he was in Millom, went on Mr. Irving, he was non-resident at the Vicarage, but he was very fortunate in having tenants like Mr. and Mrs. C. Coade. The number of preachers and visitors to the church who had been entertained by Mr. and Mrs. C. Coade on behalf of the Vicar was innumerable. He had to thank them for all their kindness. He also wanted to thank all the congregation for their loyalty. It would be impossible for him to mention all the names of those who had helped him, just as it would have been impossible for him to get along without their generous assistance.

JACKDAWS AND CHIMNEYS

It was a very wonderful and generous gift that they had now given him. He was quite sure no vicar of any parish ever received a more generous gift. He would need no reminder of Millom, but he would treasure that gift and it would bring back many happy memories. There would be a warm welcome at St. Stephen's Vicarage for any Millom friends who cared to go there. He had sometimes wondered what it was like to go into a house of one's own. Now he knew from experience. All the drains were choked, all the pipes were corroded and all the chimneys had been well stopped up by jackdaws. From one chimney they had taken a nest which was twelve feet in depth.

In conclusion, Mr. Irving mentioned that he had met their new Vicar, the Rev. P. A. Stewart, in Mesopotamia. At that time both were chaplains with the 3rd Composite Indian Division. He could say that Mr. Stewart was a very genuine and conscientiously- minded man. He hoped they would work as well with Mr. Stewart as they had done with himself, and that the parish would grow in strength more and more. The Bishop of Barrow had told him only recently that he believed Church life was really strong in Millom. Such a good gathering that night was a fine augury, and he hoped the work in Millom would prosper.

During the course of the evening a most enjoyable concert programme was given by a number of the best local artistes. Mrs. E. Bond was very successful with her soprano solos. "The Spring Hour" and "Valley of Laughter" being perhaps best. Miss A. Gilchrist gave a pleasing rendering of "The Bailiff's Daughter of Uslington," while Mr. Vincent Currie was heard to advantage in "Brian." Miss W. Woodend sang nicely, her best song being "Fairings," Mr. T. Wall gave an excellent rendering of "Sympathy" and other songs, while he and Mr. Currie rendered the duet "Watchman, what of the night?" Mr. Geo. Park was accompanist. Mr. E. Foxon gave a clever and very enjoyable oriental conjuring and illusionist display.

The Millom Gazette – Friday, November 21st 1924

INSTITUTION OF THE REV. P. A. STEWART

ADDRESS BY THE BISHOP OF BARROW

The Institution and Induction of the Rev. Philip Andrew Stewart, M.A., "to the Vicarage and Parish of Millom" took place on Saturday afternoon at the Parish Church, in the presence of a good number of parishioners. The right Rev. the Bishop of Barrow-in-Furness (the Rev. Campbell West Watson) and the Rural Dean (Rev. J. W. Akam, Seascale), by whom the charges and exhortations were made, were accompanied by the following clergy:- Revs. W. Copeland (Irton), J. F. Walton (Nether Wasdale and Wasdale Head), W. S. Sherwen (Thwaites), H. Smith (Ulpha), W. P. Ingledow (Whicham), H. J. Kendall (St. Luke's, Haverigg), J. Rowland (curate, St. George's, Millom), E. King (curate, Holy Trinity Parish Church). Messrs. W. S. Watson and G. H. Scott (churchwardens) were also present, bearing their wands of office.

The Millom Gazette – Wednesday, December 24th 1924

1925

MARRIAGE OF MILLOM VICAR

STEWART – BORRETT. On June 17th, 1925, at Christ Church, Westbourne, Bournemouth, by the Rev. Y. D. Stewart, M.A. (brother of the bridegroom), assisted by the Rev. T. H. Lingley, B.A., Vicar of the parish, the Rev. Philip Andrew Stewart, M.A., M.C., Hon. C.F., third son of the late Rev. Charles Edward Stewart, M.A., and Vicar of Millom, Cumberland, to Ruth, second daughter of Surgeon-Captain G. G. Borrett, R.N. (retired) and Mrs. Borrett, Westbourne, Bournemouth.

As announced elsewhere in this issue, the Rev. P. A. Stewart, M. A. (Vicar of Millom) was on Wednesday married to a Westbourne lady at Bournemouth. The Rev. Canon Townley (of Newby Bridge) was the preacher at Millom Parish Church last Sunday, and will conduct further services during the Vicar's absence. We understand the Rev. Mr. Stewart and his bride are spending their honeymoon in Scotland.

The Millom Gazette – Friday, June 19th 1925

1926

SOME NOTES ON MILLOM PARISH CHURCH

The parishioners of Millom seem to have been very charitable people in the past, as the records of collections for needy persons and causes show.

1665: collection "William Brocklebank, who lost his kiln by fir, vii s.," "Church in Poland and Bohemia, xiii s. ix d.," "For Margery Barben, widow, cast out of her Estate in Drumon, Ireland, vi s. vi. d."

1659: "For the inhabitants of Heydon in Yorks. that had their town destroyed by fire accidently (sic.), 6/6."

1669: "A collection for George Burkles, having suffered a great loss by fire, gathered in the parish church of Millom, 2/1."

It is an interesting fact to note that out of the first 529 baptisms there were but 12 illegitimate children, which is said to point to the good morals of the earlier inhabitants of Millom. What, it nay be asked, were the most popular name which fond parents bestowed upon their offspring? Among the boys, first and foremost, is John, closely followed by Willam and Thomas; among the girls Elizabeth, then Anne and Margaret.

Millom Gazette – Friday, April 9th 1926

1927

VICAR OF MILLOM PARISH CHURCH

ACCEPTS LIVING AT SCOTBY

Millomites generally, and Holy Trinity parishioners particularly, learned with regret last week-end that the Vicar, the Rev. P. A. Stewart, M. A. C.F., had resigned the living and accepted the offer of the living of Scotby, Carlisle (vacant by the resignation of the Rev. H. G. Rogers). The Rev. P. A. Stewart came to Millom from Shap in 1924, and has conducted the ministerial duties of the scattered Millom parish single-handed.

In the current issue of the Parish Magazine the Vicar says: - "It was with rather mixed feelings that I decided to accept the offer of another living when it came. I have been among you so short a time – it is just two and a half years since my Institution to Millom. On the other hand, the living of Scotby was first offered just over three years ago, and I would have accepted the offer then, only there was one great difficulty in the way. That difficulty no longer exists, and as the trustees have repeated the invitation I have decided, this time, to take it. One of the reasons for my mixed feelings is, of course, that the Restoration problems at Millom still remains, and one knows that, until it is solved, the lot of any future Vicar will remain a very difficult one indeed. But, apart from this one outstanding difficulty, and it involved, my wife and I have spent two very happy years amongst you, and we shall not forget the many kindnesses we have received on every hand. It is, of course, a hard parish for any man, with its three churches and scattered population, but it is a very interesting parish, with the inspiration of an historic and beautiful Parish Church, and set amidst very beautiful surroundings, and it could be, and I believe it will be, a very happy sphere of work again.

Educated at Oxford, the Vicar-elect of Scotby took his B.A. degree in 1908, and his M.A. degree in 1913. He was ordained deacon in 1910 and priest in 1911 by the Bishop of Carlisle. He was curate at Kendal from 1910 to 1914. Soon after the outbreak of the Great War he joined the Royal Army Medical Corps. He served as temporary chaplain to the Forces from 1915 until 1919, being awarded the Military Cross in 1916. After the war Mr. Stewart became Vicar of Shap, and also received an appointment as honorary chaplain to the Forces.

The Millom Gazette – Friday, May 27th 1927

REV. P. A. STEWART'S DEPARTURE

The Rev. P. A. Stewart (Vicar of Millom Holy Trinity Church), who recently accepted the living at Scotby, has been compelled, owing to exigences in his new parish, to bring his ministry in Millom to a rather unexpectedly abrupt termination, and will preach his farewell sermons on Sunday next, June 26th.

The Millom Gazette – Friday, June 24th 1927

NEW VICAR FOR MILLOM

The Rev. W. J. Phythian-Adams (of St. Mary's Church, Wellingborough) has accepted the living of the Parish of Holy Trinity, Millom, and the induction is expected to take place early next month. The Rev. A. S. Picton (from the Parish Church, Warrington) has been appointed curate, and, consequent upon the latter appointment, the Parochial Church Council have decided to resume collections in aid of the Curacy Fund, which has been suspended during recent years.

The Rev. gentleman visited the parish and attended Divine Service at Holy Trinity Church on Sunday last.

During the month of August the services of the parish are being undertaken by the Rev. Edgar Jackson, Vicar of St. John's, Sunderland

The Millom Gazette – August 5th 1927

NEW MILLOM VICAR

The Rev. W. J. T. Phythian-Adams, M.A. to whom the Bishop, as patron, has offered the Vicarage of Holy Trinity, Millom, has, as briefly announced in our last issue, accepted the offer. The new incumbent, who is curate of St. Mary's, Wellingborough, was educated at Oxford, took his B.A. degree in 1911, and proceeded to his M.A. degree in 1914. He was ordained deacon in 1925, and priest in the following year, by the Bishop of Peterborough. Before taking Holy Orders he served in the Army, being awarded the Military Cross in 1917 and the Distinguished Service Order in the following year. The vacancy at Millom is caused through the transfer of the Rev. P. A. Stewart to the Vicarage of Scotby.

The Millom Gazette – August 12th 1927

1928

INDUCTION OF FORMER MILLOM VICAR

The Rev. R. D. Ellwood (late Vicar of Whittingham, Northumberland, and formerly Vicar of Holy Trinity Church, Millom) was inducted to the living of St. Mary's, Carlisle, on Tuesday

The Millom Gazette – Friday, May 11th 1928

1929

DEATH OF PARISH CLERK

CHURCH PEOPLE'S TRIBUTE TO MR. W. H. KITCHIN

TWENTY-NINE YEARS IN OFFICE

Succeeding his father in the office of sexton and parish clerk of Holy Trinity Church, Millom, Mr. William Henry Kitchin, who passed away on Friday last, had fulfilled his duties under six Vicars during the course of twenty-nine years.

Mr. Kitchin, his father and his brother had all engaged in the work of travelling tailors, going from farm to farm in pursuit of that occupation. They represented a class of craftsman rapidly dying out, and it is some years since Mr. W. H. Kitchin ceased to engage in a trade which had made his family and himself familiar figures among the farmers of the district.

The late Mr. Kitchin had been in failing health for a considerable time before his demise, which followed an illness lasting a fortnight. He was 76 years of age.

THE FUNERAL

A fully choral funeral service was held at the church on Monday, the Rev. J. Phythian-Adams officiating. The hymns "For ever with the Lord" and "Abide with me" were sung, also Psalm 90 was chanted and Mrs. D. Hawkrigg, who presided at the organ, rendered a funeral march. Mr. W. J. Davis was the choirmaster.

Amongst the mourners were: Mr. R. Kitchin, Mr. T. Kitchin, Miss Mary Kitchin, Mrs. L. Fairclough, Miss Margery Kitchin (nephews and nieces), Mr. G. Bowness, Mrs. M. Sharpe, Mrs. Blamire, Miss D. Blamire, Miss Watson, Miss Johnson, Mr. H. J. Kirby, with many officials and members of the congregation and other friends.

Floral tributes included those of the Rev. D. W. Irving, of Carlisle, a former Vicar; the Rev. P. A. Stewart, of Scotby, who preceded the Rev. Phythian-Adams, and Mrs. Stewart; Mr. W. S. and Miss E. Watson.

Messrs. W. S. Watson, H. G. Scott (churchwardens), T. Cranke, H. Jenkinson (sidesmen), R. Kitchin and T. Kitchin (nephews) were the bearers and Mr. L. Fairclough carried out the funeral arrangements.

The Millom Gazette – March 8th 1929

HOLY TRINITY DEDICATION FESTIVAL

Holy Trinity Church, Millom held its dedication festival on Trinity Sunday, the church being well filled at all services.

A new feature was the decoration of the old church for this occasion, and this was much appreciated by members of the congregation.

The special preacher at Evensong was the Rev. W. P. Ingledow, Rector of Whicham, who spoke of the mystery of the Holy Trinity, and the need for the dedication of our lives to the glory of God.

It is interesting to note that Mr. Ingledow, who was at one time assistant curate at the Old Church, ascended its pulpit for the first time in the year 1889.

The Millom Gazette – Friday, May 31st 1929

MILLOM PARISH CHURCH

WANTED.—CARETAKER & GRAVE-DIGGER (Churchman) for above. Wage, 16/- per week. Free house and Garden. Also average annual fees, £17.—Apply, by letter only, to the VICAR by 20th June.

The Millom Gazette – Friday, June 14th 1929

IMPERIAL WAR GRAVES COMMISSION
HEADSTONES ERECTED AT HOLY TRINITY

Imperial War Graves Commission stones obtained through the agency of the Millom Branch of the British Legion, have been placed in Holy Trinity Churchyard over the graves of the following:-

Pte H. Picton, King's Liverpool Regiment, aged 44 years.

Pte. H. Kendall, Royal Lancashire Regiment, died 8th Sept., 1914, aged 18 years.

Pioneer William J. Mackereth, Royal Engineers, died 1st November, 1918, aged 19 years.

Pte. W. Martindale, Royal Lancashire Regt., died 26th Sept., 1914.

Pte. T. H. Tyson, Royal Lancashire Regt., died 11th November, 1918, aged 32 years.

Efforts are being made to secure other stones, and relatives of those who died through war service and are buried at home should communicate with the Secretary of the British Legion at Millom, Mr. H. Chapple, Newton Street.

The Millom Gazette – Friday, August 2nd 1929

HOLY TRINITY CHURCH, MILLOM – PRE 1930

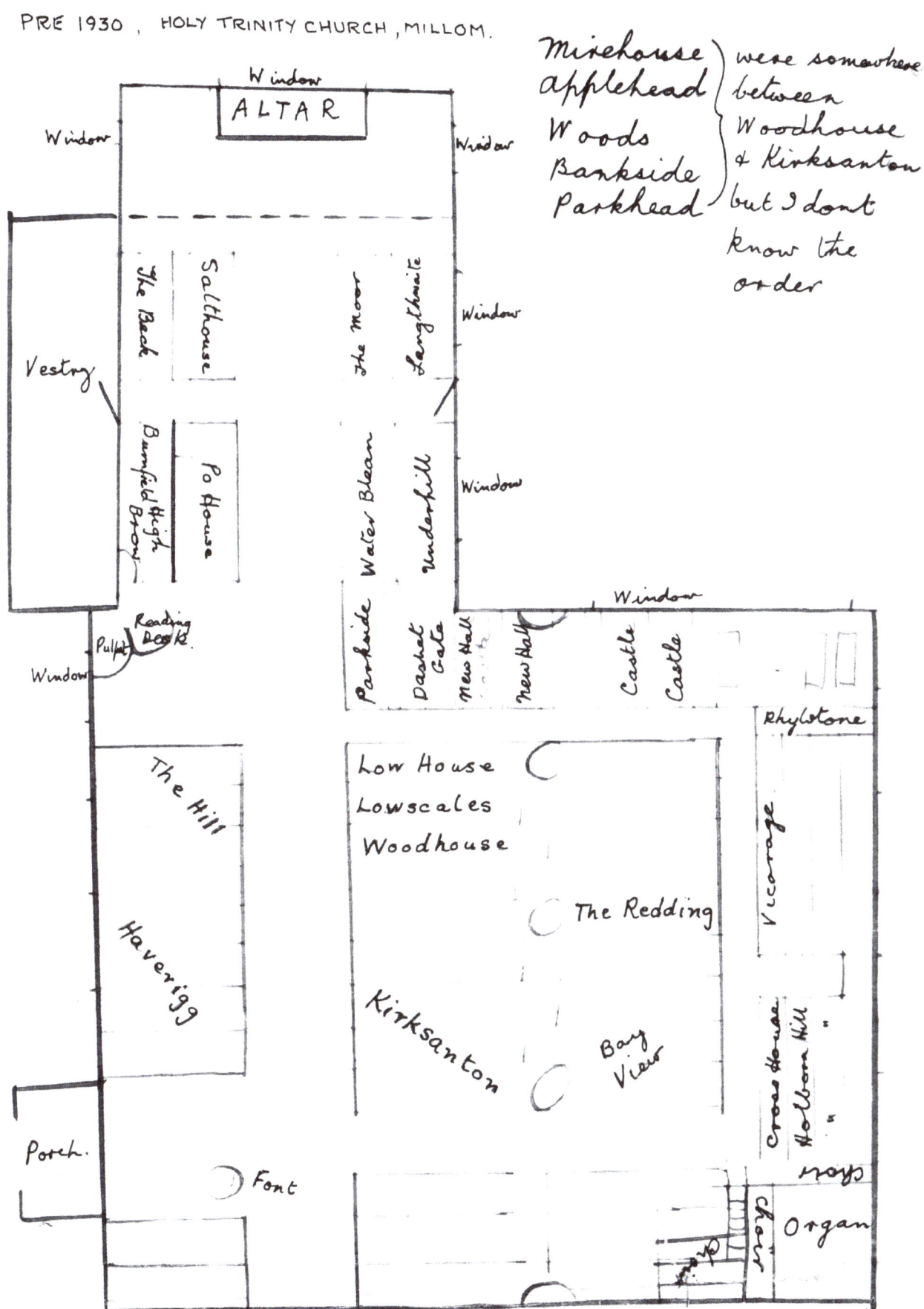

Image © Millom Heritage & Arts Centre

THE CHURCH OF THE HOLY TRINITY, MILLOM
THE LIFE-STORY OF A HOLY PLACE

We are indebted to the Rev. W. J. Phythian-Adams (Vicar) for the following article (the first of a series) relating to the Holy Trinity Church, Millom:-

It may be of interest to some of our readers to follow in imagination the life and growth of the Church. Admittedly we have to rely to a large extent on conjecture, and perhaps during the work we hope to carry out we shall find evidence which disproves some of our guesses. But what we may lose in that way will be more than compensated by the interest of thinking out the various steps in the life of the Old Church, and as no one will be a whit the worse for any mistakes in guessing that we make, we can start on our romantic voyage without alarm. We begin naturally with

BIRTH

I am beginning to be pretty sure that when our Church was born she was a Saxon, that is that she began life before William the Conqueror's invasion of England in 1066. Moreover, like any other highly respectable person she began as a baby of small, simple, and not very beautiful appearance, and she looked like this:-

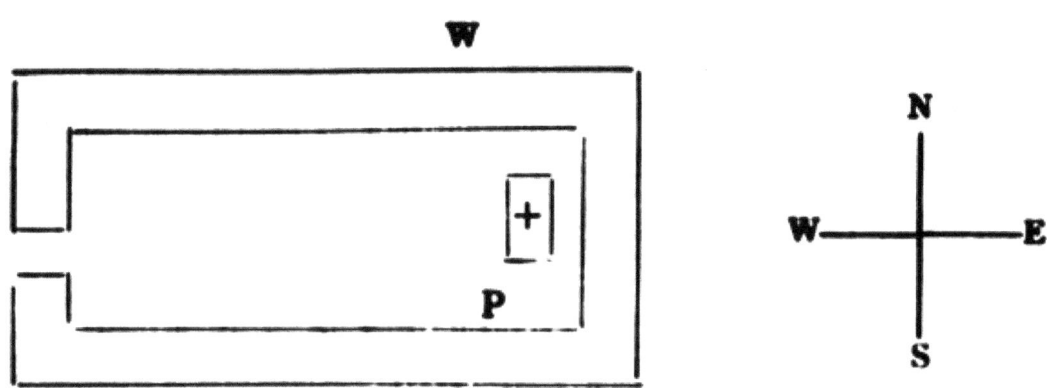

In other words, what first stood on this spot was a small rectangular chapel with the door at the West end and the altar (of course) at the East. In the South Wall by the Altar (P on the Plan) were the Piscina down which the water and wine used for cleansing the chalice were poured and the Aumbrey or small cupboard in which the sacred vessels were locked when not in use. There would, of course, be no chairs or proper flooring, the congregation for the most part standing, or of not, kneeling on the rushes strewn beneath their feet. I have only put in one of the windows (W on the Plan). Naturally there would be others all round, but this one is the one that interests us because it is there to this day where I have marked it: just as the old Piscina and the very rough and primitive Aumbrey are there for anyone to see in the South Wall by the altar.

You will by this time have recognised this baby. It is simply our present Chancel with a west wall and door where the chancel arch now is, and very narrow slit-like windows in place of the present East window, the Irving Memorial window and the other two. The present "priests' door" in the south wall would not yet have been needed, so it would not have been in existence.

Naturally there is some dispute as to whether there are any parts of the Church older than the Norman period (from 1066 to about 1190), so we must not take our guess for granted. Mr. Ellwood, in his little book about the Church, thinks that the base of the old cross by the sundial in the Churchyard may be pre-Norman in date, though, on the other hand, he is doubtful about our window (W). I think, however, there is another way of approaching this point. In the first place, the present Chancel seems very clearly to be a single whole in itself. The western part of the Church was almost certainly tacked on to it at a later date, as we shall see. When that happened, the old Chapel became the Chancel of the new and larger church, as it has been ever since. You only have to look at it to see that it is much too long to have been built originally as the Chancel.

There were no choirs in those days, and all that was needed of a Chancel was space for the Altar and Sanctuary: quite a short projection from the nave of the church eastwards was sufficient. If, then, our present chancel was not built as a chancel, it must have existed before as a chapel "in its own right," as it were. But if it had been built by the Normans it would almost certainly have had a rounded east-end (an apse) instead of the square rectangular end that we see to-day. It is, of course, possible that somewhere underneath or near the foot of the present east wall, we may find traces of a Norman Apse, in which case we shall know where we are. The Norman Lord of the Castle might well have turned his master-mason on to the building of a chapel after the completion of the Castle itself. However, up to the present there are no traces of an apse, and as it is one of the characteristics of small "Saxon" (i.e., Pre-Norman) churches to have square, and nor rounded, east ends (it was easier to build them like that) we may very well suppose that our own is a case in point and that our Church first saw the light of day before the Conquest. How much remains of the actual structure one cannot of course say: there are old window-heads (built into the present south wall of the Chancel) which apparently belonged to the earliest church. Presumably when the present windows were inserted there was a good deal of pulling down and rebuilding, as there must always be when improvements of any kind are made. But I feel pretty confident that the foundations of all three walls are the early and original foundations of the Church of the Holy Trinity, Millom   W. J. P. A

The Millom Gazette – Friday, October 4th 1929

THE LIFE-STORY OF A HOLY PLACE (2)

Having attended the infant Church at her birth, we can now pass in due course to her

CHILDHOOD.

This I take to be represented by her Norman remains. After the Conquest a Castle of some kind seems to have been built on the present site. That means two things, an increase in population on the very doorstep of the Church, and the arrival of a new Lord of The Manor with more wealth and considerably more culture than his old Saxon predecessors. That in turn meant a larger church and some attempt at decorative effect. The present North door, with its typical round arch and its simple embellishments, represents the second of these: the "larger church" presented a more difficult problem. Generally, the Normans liked to make their churches in the shape of the Cross, with the short arms projecting to north and south at the point where the Chancel joined on to the Nave. This is not, of course, an invariable rule, and it is easy to see why in the case of Millom Church it was not followed. To begin with, the old Chapel (if our guess is correct) was already standing there to be used as the Chancel of the new Church. As we have seen, it was really far too long to be convenient for that purpose, but to shorten it meant a good deal of not very useful labour, and that would determine the new-comers to leave it as it was. That being so, however, it could not be used as the top end of a normal cross-shaped Church, because to make the arms and, still more, the long foot of such a Cross in anything like true proportion would have meant building a larger Nave and larger Transepts than could ever have been required at that time of scattered and comparatively scanty population. Moreover, if the moat was in existence then (and it is almost certain to have been dug out when the first Castle was built) there would have been no room for the northern arm of the Cross, and the cruciform design would not therefore have been carried out. All this may serve to explain why the Norman church followed the lines it did and brought the enlargement of the building to its next stage:-

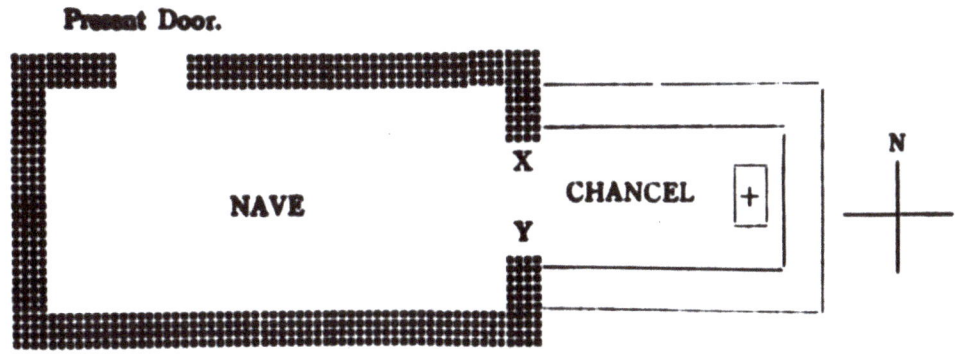

A glance at this diagram will show at once the simplicity of the new Scheme. Between the points X and Y the west wall of the old Chapel was pulled down, enough of this wall being left projecting on both sides to support the new round Chancel arch (as on the north side it still does). The north and south walls of the new Nave started by just over-lapping the outside of the old chapel walls, and the new door was provided in its present position at the west end of the north wall. It was natural to put it in this position, and not in the west or south walls, because this made it more handy for the Castle folk, who were, of course, responsible for the enlargement. Perhaps they used the extra length of the Chancel as a sort of Castle-pew where they could sit and worship in state while the humble fry crowded in the new Nave.

Of the windows of this Church no trace now remains. Those at present in the north and west walls are terrible examples of Victorian "restoration." Perhaps some of our older people may have heard tell what kind of windows these new ones replaced. Were they similar in general shape to these, or were they more like the windows of the Hudleston Chapel? If they were the former, then the strong probability is that they were the original old Norman windows of the new Nave, in which case it is all the more regrettable that they have been so completely destroyed. Fortunately in these later times we have learned our lesson, and every such ancient feature of an old Church like ours is preserved as jealously as if it were made of gold.

Several interesting events in the Childhood of the Church deserves to be mentioned. It was in or about the year 1220 (Mr. Ellwood tells us) that "William son of Hugh" made a grant "to God and the Abbey of Holy Mary of Furness of the Church of the Holy Trinity of Millom with the chapels, lands and tenements, and all other their appurtenances." By this time also, we are told, there was a Wednesday market at Millom (i.e., presumably at the Castle, as there was no town of that name) and a three-day Fair in the week following the Feast of the Holy Trinity. The grant of the Church to the Abbey is of great importance, for the Abbey thereby became the Rector, and as such took over sole charge and possession of the Chancel. The result of this change will become apparent at the next stage. The fair at Holy Trinity Tide is an extremely interesting proof of the very early dedication of our Church to that Most Glorious Name. Finally, the mention of a market makes it clear that the neighbourhood was becoming more populous, and gives us a further good reason for the enlargement of the building.   W. J. P. A

The Millom Gazette – Friday, October 11th 1929

THE LIFE-STORY OF A HOLY PLACE (3)

YOUTH.

Childhood is a stage of life marked by simplicity of mind and body. With Youth – if we may use that name to describe the years that stretch between Childhood and Middle Age – there comes to most people an immense change. They find suddenly in life a new thrill, a new buoyancy, a sense of Romance, a feeling after Adventure, a yearning to do something big on as big a scale as possible. In England, and particularly in the history of English architecture, the 13th and 14th centuries are saturated with this spirit of youth. If we do not realise this at the outset, the next stage in the life-story of our Church will remain incomprehensible. Let me mention only two things as illustrations of this extraordinary exuberance which bubbled up like champagne and made our master-craftsmen almost drunk with the joy of new adventure. The old sober round-headed Norman arches and the round and massive pillars on which they rested had, and still have, a solemn beauty of their own; but when the pointed Gothic arch was discovered and, with it, the slender columns and piers which were found strong enough to do all the work of the old masses of masonry while adding enormously to the delicate beauty of the building, the imagination of our English masons soared away towards Heaven and broke out upon a delighted world, in a whole series of lofty Churches and Abbeys and glorious Cathedrals. In a little country Church like our own you cannot, of course, see that spirit in its strength, and yet it has been there at work all the same. The pillars which support the central arcade must have been thought miracles of slender beauty to Millom folk when they were first displayed. Indeed, when the proper level of the Church is recovered, and we gain once more the vision of its true proportions, we ourselves are quite certainly going to be astonished and delighted at the change. But that is only a small point. It is the size of the Hudleston Chapel and what seems at first glance the wholly unnecessary spaciousness of its great East window which are the surest indications of the spirit of England's youth.

When you remember that in addition to that enormous window, there are no less than three other large ones in the South wall, you are bound to feel at first that the thing is overdone. Not a bit of it! You are forgetting the stained glass. It was no mere rioting after size for its own sake that these old master-builders were displaying. It is perfectly true that they did revel in huge and lofty spaces, just as they liked experimenting in odd shapes (witness our own "Fish" window, though that has its symbolic meaning). But they revelled also in colour. The acres of window-glass that you see in Gothic Churches and Cathedrals of this date (from the early part of the 14th century) were intended to display the glories of the Gospel story and the triumphs of the saints in every variety of colour and subject and design. But beauty, when it is artificial, has to be paid for, and in this case it could only be had at the expense of daylight. What was the solution? Clearly, if you wanted tour windows filled with deeply-coloured stained-glass, you must make them an "outsize" or you would leave your Church in the dimness of a perpetual twilight. That is by far the most probable explanation of the large and numerous windows of the Hudleston Chapel, every detail of which links it with one of the most glorious and inspiring periods of English Gothic architecture.

It is time now to consider what happened at the new enlargement:-

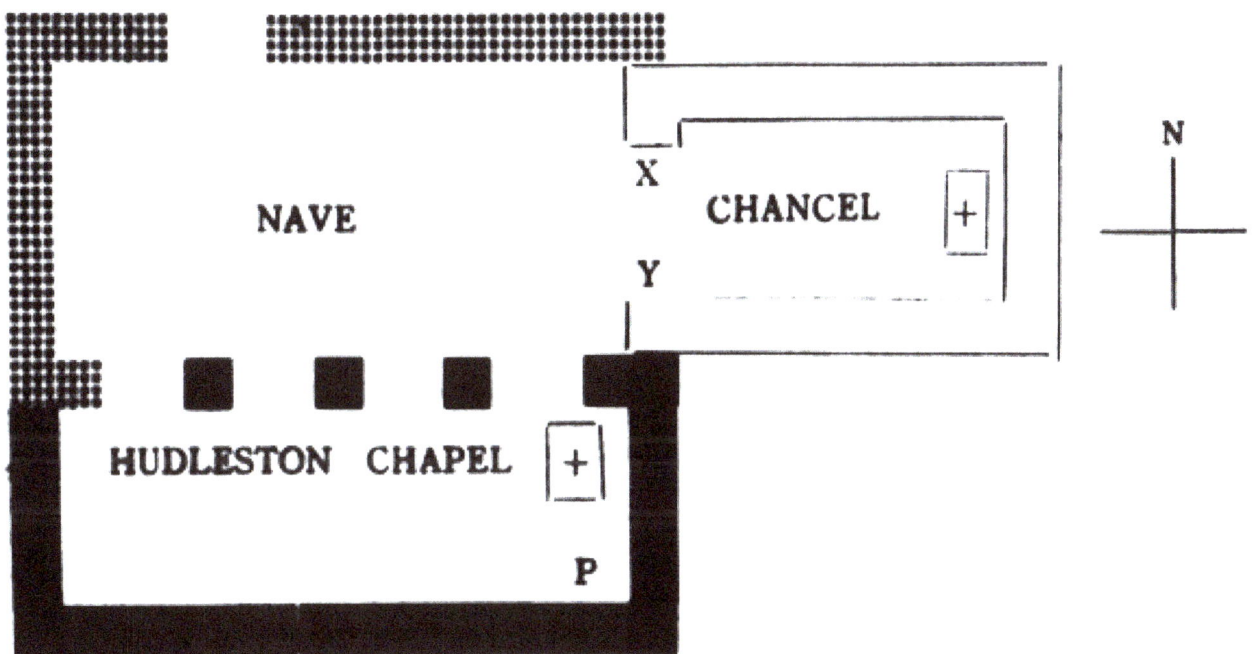

If you will compare this with the other two diagrams, particularly the second, you will see without difficulty what the Hudlestons did when they built their new chantry on to the South of the old Nave. They pulled down almost the whole of the (Norman) South wall, windows and all: in fact, except for a small projection at its West end (intended to support their new pointed arch at this point) they destroyed it entirely and put their arcade of three columns in its place. At its east end, where it overlapped the original Chapel, now the Chancel, they had to do away, as well, with a portion of the old Chapel's south wall, (Point Y on the diagram). They were going to put in their great East window just to the South of it, and it is probable that they thought it wiser to make their own new central pier at this point to combine the thrust both of this window and the chancel arch. This, of course, is simply a guess: but the fact remains that they did destroy this part of the of the old Chapel wall and that they readjusted the Chancel Arch so as to make it spring from their new pier. It is impossible to believe that they really meant to leave things like that. If you look at the Chancel arch as it stands now, you will see that it is in line with nothing at all: it is central neither to the Chancel (as it must once have been) nor to the Nave. Apart from this, the fact that the Nave and Hudleston Chapel roofs are noticeably higher than that of the Chancel (a change no doubt made at the same time), has left a very unsightly boarded space, which catches everybody's eye, immediately under the Chancel Arch. Lastly, the old south wall of the Chancel, where it was cut off at the point Y, has a peculiarly bare, unfinished, ugly look. We may be sure that the men who built the new arcade and put in those wonderful windows in the new Chantry never intended that the Chancel, the most important part of the

Church, should remain so dwarfed and so disfigured in comparison with the remainder of the building. There can be little doubt that they hoped to persuade the Rector (who, as we have seen, was then the Abbey of Furness) to undertake the work of widening and heightening the Chancel (the Rector's charge and special possession) so that it might not fall behind or be shamed by the glory and spaciousness of the new enlargements. Why this never happened we hope to explain later.   W. J. P. A.

The Millom Gazette – Friday, October 18th 1929

THE LIFE-STORY OF A HOLY PLACE (4)
MIDDLE AGE.

The reason why nothing more was done to the Parish Church after the new Hudleston enlargements is almost a tragic one; and it is a tragedy not of Millom only but of all England. It is the outbreak of that appalling pestilence which men learned to call under their breath the Black Death (1348-1349). This is not the place to dwell upon the horrors of it and the frightful havoc and desolation that it left behind. We need only realise that when the plague passed, and men dared to think again of life and happiness, there were many old hopes and plans and many fair and pleasant prospects which never revived to gladden a new generation. From that day onwards the Old Church remained to all practical purposes as she was, save that the years rolled by relentlessly and left their mark behind. Windows got blocked up, a new south door was opened, and then, in a blocked window, yet another. The old roof must have been restored and lowered at some unknown date, for the present one is not of very great age (late 17th century?) though in its quaint workmanship it remains to this day one of the finest features in the building. It has been suggested that it once had tie-beams across the Nave and Hudleston Chapel, and that these were cut through and removed when the ceilings were taken down. This, however, can hardly be correct. A ceiling there certainly has been, as anyone can see; but the roof itself has been constructed for the most part without the usual tie-beams. Was it perhaps (as a friend has suggested) the work of some old local shipwright? It is very cheering to hear that so far the timbers have escaped the dreaded evil of dry-rot, but we shall have to remember that we cannot hope to avoid this in the future unless we take steps to guard against it now.

Of other changes that have taken place, the Hudleston Chapel has been the chief sufferer. Before the Reformation it had, of course, its own Altar at which Mass was said by the Chantry Priest for the repose of the souls of departed Hudlestons. The piscina of this altar (P. on the diagram) is still to be seen in its old place in the south wall of the Chapel. At the Reformation this Altar would have been instantly removed, and it was then perhaps that the two Hudleston tombs were bundled away together into the corner where they now are. Considering what this Parish owes to the family, we might well make it part of our duty to remove this rather ugly, if unconscious, suggestion of indifference and neglect.

Another alteration which may have taken place at this period resulted (in all probability) from the threatened collapse of the old West wall of the Nave. When people try to put on weight on a structure not built to stand it, something has to give! In this case we may suppose that it was the weight of a new bell-cote (not, of course, the present one, which is quite modern) which began to produce ominous signs of cracking and yielding in the ancient wall beneath it. The danger of a complete collapse seems to have been averted by the insertion of the curious stone arch for which so many attempted explanations have been given. That this was ever a doorway seems to the present writer, with all respect to other people's opinions, quite incredible. Its shape alone would have necessitated as queer a door as man ever set eyes on; while, on the other hand, the wide splay of it is just what you would expect if it is just what you would expect if it was intended to relieve the strain of the new weight imposed above it. The wall itself was saved, but it is impossible to admire the resulting effect, for the work seems to have been done with great haste and in a very careless and, indeed, slovenly manner. The Northern half of our present West wall is, in fact, NOT one of the glories of our church, and I suppose most of us try to avoid looking at its outside when we pass it! It is not for us to pass judgement on godly men of the past, but one cannot help feeling that when the West window had to be restored in the 19th century the ugly features of this wall might well have been dealt with at the same time. Perhaps, however, that task, too, had been reserved for us.

I have not attempted, as you will see, to treat this period in details, for the very good reason that we know next to nothing about it. When the vestry was built; when the priest's door and the new windows in the

South wall of the Chancel were opened (the westernmost is, of course, a comparatively modern one, and not a real Church window at all); these and other like problems excite our interest only to baffle it.

But this was a fine period in our Church's life-story, a fine one and a long one. Our registers begin in it, and, with them, a growing sense of real Parochial life, even though the boundaries of the Parish ran up to Ulpha. It is Middle Age, but a hale and hearty Middle Age, for it is the age of Shakespeare and the great Elizabethan Captains of the Sea. Some whisper of their doings must surely have reached to far-off Millom: some echo of Drake's Drum must have come to it over the Main; and though these things, of themselves, had little religion in them, yet they breathed the fresh air of a new Faith and a new Age which we who worship within those same walls to-day, may well remember and, it may be, regain.   W. J. P. A.

The Millom Gazette – Friday, October 25th 1929

THE LIFE-STORY OF A HOLY PLACE (5)

OLD AGE.

The 18th and 19th Centuries were a period of Old Age for the entire Church of England, and the reason is not far to seek. The living voice of the Church, Convocation, was suppressed: her offices were filled largely by political appointment: on all sides Religion was divested of all sense of awe and mystery, and became a dreary round of droned prayers and interminable sermons. At St. Paul's Cathedral in the year 1800 there were but six communicants at the only Celebration on Easter Day! After this we need not be astonished at the present state of our Chancel. The tragic failure of the past to complete the enlargement and beautification of the Sanctuary conspired to encourage its neglect. At a time when the Holy Table and the Holy Mysteries celebrated at it were all too little thought of, in our own Church the very building itself cast them still further into the background. The more the pulpit bulked in the eyes of all beholders, the more the long and narrow Chancel receded from their thoughts, till it became little more than pew-space for the surplus congregation. In the body of the Church the same over-empasis (sic.) on the pulpit has destroyed itself even more clearly. The Hudleston Chapel, stript of its altar and thus deprived of its proper focus for devotion at its east end, has become choked with pews which face northwards towards the preacher. With (sic.) this arrangement was first made it is impossible to say. The present pitch pine pews (Mr. Ellwood tells us) were substituted for the old oak benches in 1858, so that we know nothing about the position of the seating before then. One thing, however, we must not forget. Slowly as the population increased in the 18th and early 19th centuries, it was all the time steadily outgrowing the seating accommodation of the old Parish Churches. When we remember that what was not long ago the single Parish of Millom is now served by three Parish Churches and three "Chapels-of-Ease" (not to mention the place of worship attended by our Nonconformist brethren) we can understand the need for crowding the Old Church with pews and, after all that, for adding a gallery at the west end to take the overflow. Even quite recently when any Restoration Scheme was submitted, it was a necessary condition that the seating accommodation must not be diminished as a result of it. To-day the Authorities are less inclined to enforce these terms. They realise, with all other educated Churchmen, that it is just this overcrowding with pews that has choked the spirit of worship in the Church of England in the past, and that the very seats which were once thought so precious will, if they are left, remain empty and unused for ever, an eye-sore to everybody, a benefit to none.

To this same period of Old Age we have to attribute one special grievous alteration, the raising of the floor level by nearly two feet. Let it be admitted that there was a highly practical reason for this, the dampness of the old flagged floor: yet the fact remains that this alteration should at all costs have been avoided. The whole beauty of a simple building, such as ours, consists in its proportions, and if you disturb these you deprive it of more than half its charm. Let it be remembered that a step in this wrong direction had already been taken when the roofs of the Nave of Hudleston Chapel were lowered. This alteration not merely cut off a clear view of the top of the chancel arch, but it brought the roof much nearer to the old floor than the master-masons of the 14th century had ever intended. To that extent, then, their proportions had already been upset, and a corresponding loss of spaciousness and loftiness had been the penalty. To increase this loss still further by bringing the floor, in its turn, nearer the roof can only be described as lamentable. It has cramped the whole building and given it an entirely undeserved atmosphere of closeness and stuffiness which must affect – even though unconsciously – all those who habitually worship in it.

Strangely enough too, the raising of the floor has proved ineffective. The damp has now risen, undeterred by those two feet, and is now clinging to the mattings as if they belonged to it!

We close our survey of this period without regret. It is never pleasing to dwell on an age of stagnation and decay, and our only purpose in considering it at all has been that we may learn from it some lessons that may help us in the days that lie ahead. It would be unfair, however, to end on such a note. Towards the close of the 19th century a new spirit began to assert itself in the Church of England, and our Church bears witness to is presence. The restorations which proceeded from it are not, perhaps, such as would command our unstinted admiration to-day: yet restoration and beautification of any kind are evidence of interest and affection which we do well to reverence. When men love their old Church; when it hurts them to see her disfigured and ill-adorned; when they set themselves with all their might and with the best artistic knowledge at their disposal to restore her beauty and make her worthy of her sacred purpose, then the miracle of that Church's undying life is once more seen in operation. Before Love, Old Age shrinks back defeated, and the glow of life returns. W. J. P. A.

The Millom Gazette – Friday, November 1st 1929

1930

MILLOM CHURCH ALTERATIONS

ANCIENT BUILDING WITH SOME DISTINCT PECULIARITIES

Various alterations are to be made to Millom Parish Church. The Chancellor in granting a faculty at Carlisle, yesterday, said the church was a very ancient one and presented some distinct peculiarities. There was a narrow chancel with a low roof, and the nave had been widened on the south side. The church fell into disrepair during the 18th century, and was put into better order in 1858, but it had been felt that judicious restoration was now required, and to be carried out in such a way as to preserve the interesting features of the place, besides making it more suitable for public worship. Considerable money had been raised for the purpose and for the purchase of an organ, which would be placed in the gallery against the west wall. The alterations would include a new vestry, widening of the chancel, the reconstruction of the chancel arch, and the formation of an entirely new roof in English oak and green slate. The alterations would also include the regrouping of two altar tombs in the Hudleston Chapel. The Chancellor congratulated the Vicar, the Rev. W. J. Phythian-Adams, and the Parochial Church Council upon having agreed to such an excellent and comprehensive scheme of church restoration.

The Lancashire Daily Post – Thursday, April 10th 1930

MILLOM PARISH CHURCH

FACULTY GRANTED FOR RECONSTRUCTION

The Rev. W. Phythian-Adams, D.S.O., M.C., Vicar of Millom, was at Carlisle Consistory Court on Tuesday granted a faculty to reconstruct the ancient Millom Parish Church.

Chancellor Campbell, in granting the faculty, said the restoration would preserve most of what was old and interesting in the church, and would make many improvements.

The additions will include a new vestry and organ, and a new heating system

The Millom Gazette – Friday, April 11th 1930

CORRESPONDENCE

THE OLD PARISH CHURCH

(To the Editor of the "Millom Gazette").

Sir, - You have been kind enough to print a series of short historical notes on the development of the Old Parish Church, and the fact that these have drawn to me correspondence even from distant parts encourages me to ask you to print this appeal to all past and present worshippers in this venerable building.

I endeavoured to show that the Church as it stands is evidently incomplete. The Hudlestons of the 14th century having erected their wide Nave and South Aisle (the "Hudleston Chapel"), made no effort to "finish off" the junction of the Chancel Arch with the old long, low and narrow Chancel to the East of it. They hoped, without doubt, that the Abbey of Furness, which was the Rector, would widen this Chancel to correspond with the new Nave. For some reason or other this work, which would have been not so much an improvement as a necessary completion of the whole enlargement of the Church, was never carried out, and the Chancel has remained as it was, eloquently unworthy of the building of which it should have been the glory.

The admirable plans which have been prepared by Messrs. Hicks & Charlewood, of Newcastle-upon-Tyne, are designed to carry on, after the lapse of so many centuries, the pious intentions of those who first enlarged the Church. All the unfinished and unsightly aspects of the chancel arch, roof and walls will disappear in an enlarged and noble Sanctuary, and that with the minimum of reconstruction and without the removal of any feature of historical or antiquarian interest. Those who are privileged to worship in the Church after the Restoration will be astonished at the extraordinary improvement accomplished with so little substantial change.

To turn to other features of our proposal:-

(a) The problem of installing a new organ in an old church where no provision, of course, exists, is notoriously a difficult one. It will be solved for us by the erection of a very simple and beautiful balustraded "minstrels" gallery at the west end of the Nave, to contain both choir and organ, and to receive its light from apertures in the roof. The design of the beautiful "Caroline" communion-rails is being followed for the balustrading of the front and staircase of this gallery, and the Organ case will be harmonised with it. The Font will be re-erected centrally underneath.

The Font in Holy Trinity Church 1930. Photo reproduced here with kind permission of Mr. D. Snell. Image © Mr. D. Snell

(b) The Hudleston Chapel will be restored to its ancient use for week-day services by a simple regrouping of the Altar Tombs and the restoration of the seats to their proper eastward aspect. The westernmost of the three windows will be opened up, and the tracery of the third will be restored. I might add that all the window-tracery will be treated with special preservative solution.

(c) Throughout the Church the original floor level will be resumed, modern damp-proof being more than capable of coping with the old evil which caused it to be raised in the last century. A dry area along the North wall will form part of this anti-damp campaign, and an improved heating system will make things doubly sure.

Space forbids me to dwell in any greater detail on our plans, but I should add that we are installing electric light from the Urban District Council, and that this will be disposed on the "flood-light" system which is now being widely used in churches and with wonderful effectiveness. This does not exhaust our list of improvements, but it will be sufficient to show that we have set our hands to a big work, and would gratefully welcome the help and encouragement of all our friends. The Chancellor has granted us the necessary Faculty, and we shall start as soon as possible: but we are faced at present with the prospect of having another £1000 to raise. I wonder whether anyone in or beyond our borders will send us a contribution, great or small, for the Glory of God and the sake of Auld Lang Syne? – I am, Sir,

    Your obedient servant,
    W. John Phythian-Adams
    Vicar of Millom.

The Millom Gazette – Friday, April 11th 1930

A SOUVENIR OF THE RESTORATION – 1930
(From the archives of Millom Heritage & Arts Centre)

THE CHURCH AS IT IS TODAY

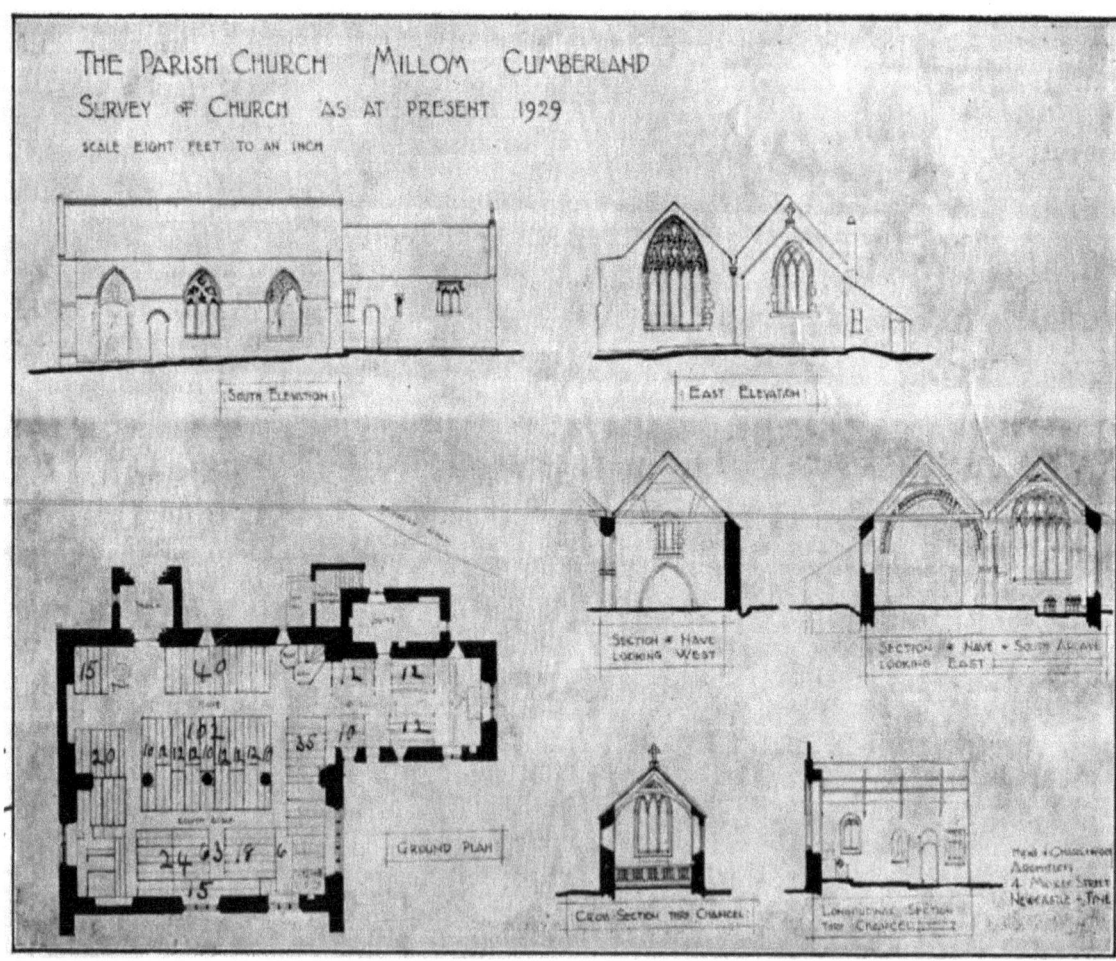

Image © Millom Heritage & Arts Centre

THE CHURCH dates back to the Norman Era (12th Century); but it is possible that the CHANCEL covers the site of a still earlier Chapel to which the De Boyvils (Lords of the Manor, 1130-1250 A. D.) added the NAVE. Of this Nave the North Wall and Door and West Wall still remain. The North Chancel Window is also of this period.

In the following Century the NAVE was enlarged by the Hudlestons (the new Lords) and the CHANCEL ARCH was built. Further improvements were clearly in view; but for some unknown reason the work was stopped and was not resumed till the 14th Century, in which the HUDLESTON CHANTRY or CHAPEL was completed with its present windows, but no attempt was made to deal with the unfinished Chancel.

Much damage is said to have been done to the building by Cromwell's artillery in 1644 and it remained in a neglected state till the restoration of 1858.

THE TOMBS. The Alabaster Tomb is probably that of Sir John Hudleston (d. 1494) and his wife Joan. The altar-tomb carries the arms of Hudleston, Leigh of Isell, Curwen, Pennington and other families with whom the Hudlestons intermarried.

THE FONT dates back to the first half of the 14th Century.

Handwritten to the left of the image of the GROUND PLAN is a list of the number of seats in the church at the time:

Chancel 46, Castle 35, Pulpit side 40, Main 102, Back 35, Side 63 = 324 without Choir

THE CHURCH AS IT WILL BE

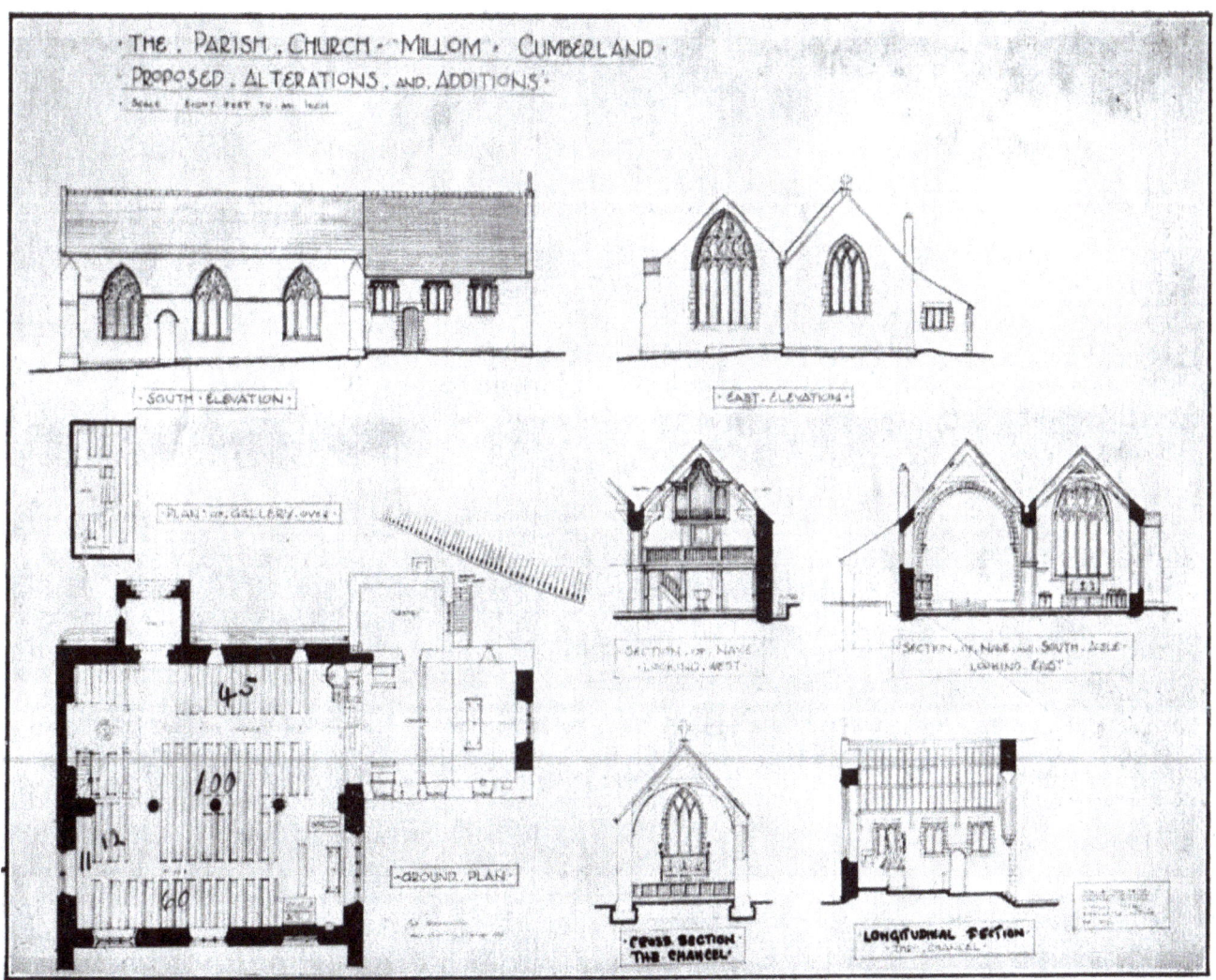

Image © Millom Heritage & Arts Centre

THE PRESENT RESTORATION is guided by two main considerations; to complete the unfinished work of the 15th Century and to place the new organ in the best position possible. All other improvements arise out of these and are dependent to them.

i. The widening of the CHANCEL and the recentering of the Arch carry out the intentions of the early Huddlestons. The unusual length of the Chancel, which makes the Altar invisible to many persons in the Church, is overcome by the moving of the Altar westwards and the advance of the (extended) Communion Rails. The two new windows similar to the existing ("Irving") window give added light and beauty to this, the most sacred part of the Church.

ii. The new ORGAN and CHOIR GALLERY at the West end of the Nave follows, in its design, the old Caroline Communion Rails. Beneath it is the Baptistery. The space previously occupied by the Choir and Organ is now available for the Congregation.

iii. The HUDLESTON CHAPEL is restored to its ancient purposes. Its westernmost window is opened for much-needed light, and the tracery of the easternmost is restored. Both here and in the Nave the original floor level is recovered and made damp-proof; and the full height of the columns, with their bases, is once more visible.

iv. The Scheme includes roof-restoration, electric light, a new heating system and a reconstructed Vestry.

MILLOM PARISH CHURCH

During the work of Restoration, which has now begun and is expected to take about five or six months, the Holy Communion will be celebrated at the Parish Mission Room, Holborn Hill. Matins and Evensong on Sundays will be sung at the Parish Church Institute (Upper Room). It is estimated that there will be room for about 150 persons.

Residents at The Hill or Kirksanton are earnestly requested to frequent their own chapel-of-ease services during this period, and to leave the Institute for worshippers of the town.

The weekly notices of services will be found outside the Parish Room, and not at the Church.

The Millom Gazette – Friday June 6th 1930

WHO WERE THEY?

Underneath the raised flooring of the Old Church was discovered a small square billet of wood, bearing the following pencilled inscription:- "Mossop Caddy and William Hindle, joiners at Millom Church, April 26th, 1859. Ja[mes?] Weeks, contractors, Bootle." Can any of our readers recognise the persons concerned? We are glad to think that this parting message of theirs has survived, as they hoped, to reach the hands of a generation 70 years later.

The Millom Gazette – Friday June 6th 1930

CORRESPONDENCE
(To the Editor of the "Millom Gazette")

Sir, - In forwarding you the accompanying report, which may be of interest to your readers, may I refer to two matters which I understand have caused some concern?

(1) It is well-known that in the course of lowering the inside level of the floor we have discovered a considerable number of mortal remains. This was not unexpected, but I hope it will be understood that none of these was found in an undisturbed burial. The loose earth which had been brought in from the Churchyard to raise the floor level in 1858 was responsible for their presence. All such relics have been decently re-interred in special graves in the Churchyard. If there have been burials inside the Church, as no doubt there have, we have not needed to excavate to their depth, and they will continue to lie where they have lain undisturbed hitherto.

(2) The other point on which I occasionally hear remarks is that it is thought regrettable that we should destroy any part of an ancient building. I should be glad if it could be widely known that the portions of the Church which we are treating most drastically, i.e., the north and south walls of the Chancel, are in no sense ancient buildings, as my Report will show. It is true that these walls have been standing on the (hidden) foundations of an older Chancel, but they themselves, so far from being of substantial or historic importance, were poorly built and of comparatively recent date. I can assure those of your

readers who did not see them in the stages of demolition that they may be allowed to disappear "unwept, unhonoured, and unsung."

Yours faithfully,
W. J. PHYTHIAN-ADAMS.
June 23rd, 1930

MILLOM PARISH CHURCH

THE FIRST STAGES OF RESTORATION

**The Church during restoration. Photo reproduced here with kind permission of Mr. D. Snell.
Image © Mr. D. Snell**

Work on the dismantling of the North and South Walls of the Chancel has gone rapidly forward, thanks partly to the poor condition of the masonry. The present writer has expressed in the past the conviction that these walls were of no great antiquity and this has been absolutely corroborated in the course of demolition. The construction almost throughout appears to have been of a somewhat slipshod character, a rubble filling having been rammed in with sandy and indifferent mortar between a thin double skin or facing of masonry. There had been scarcely any attempt to bond the walls into the east wall of the Nave under the Chancel Arch; in some places (notably under the small window in the North Wall) slates and pebbles were thrown in without any mortar at all; the piscina in the South Wall had been very roughly backed by an irregular bit of slate: in short, the work reached only a very mediocre standard. The fragment of the stem of a "churchwarden" clay pipe, found embedded in the centre of the South Wall, gives a good indication of the date of this part of the Church. At a still later date, when the wooden-framed domestic window was inserted to the west of the "priest's door," further and much ruder alterations were made. These will be noted below. The signs of reconstruction became very quickly clear as the work proceeded. It had been hoped that with the removal of the plaster we might find the freestone jambs of the doors and centre window intact. (The "Irving" Window was known to be complete already). Unfortunately, our hopes were dashed. A few chamfered blocks remained, but the greater part of the stones were of squared masonry roughly hacked to a chamfer to take a coat of plaster. In the centre window (the head of which was a thin slab of modern workmanship) the chamfer was a pure "fake": it had been cut in the plaster, and the rough wall face beneath showed nothing to correspond with it. (We may note with regret, in passing, the damage which has been done in past times to all surviving stone jambs by the pick-marking of their surface for this same inevitable plaster!). Finally, as the South Wall came down, stone after stone proved to have been reused from some older building. A small portion of a scalloped capital was found here, and also a curious carving of an orb and cross with a fragment of another cross incised to the left of it. The surface of this stone was a roughly broken one, and it is hard to believe that it ever bore an important design. Perhaps we shall find more light on it later on. From this wall, also, came a thinnish and slightly curving stone, bearing the mysterious legend ANTEF.

So far, it must be confessed, this report has nothing much of interest to offer; but we come now to matters more attractive. It has been said above that when the westernmost window in the South Wall was inserted, the masonry belonging to it, and, we may now add, below it, was of a very rough description. It consisted, in fact of a loosely built wall of unmortared stones, its true character being concealed, as usual, by the plaster. When, however, these stones fell away (for it was unnecessary to do more than give them a push), there was disclosed behind them a very curious feature. It will be remembered that as the wall stood before we began work, it presented to those seated in the nave a bare protruding square plastered face: it formed, in fact, the abrupt end of the two-feet-thick south wall. But this appearance was entirely due to the late dry-walling under the new window: it was this and this alone which completed that square protruding angle which we used to long to cut away! What was our astonishment when we found that in much earlier times it had already been cut away! Behind the dry-walling were exposed a few feet of roughly cut away wall surface, covered with a strong coating of white plaster. For a considerable time we were completely puzzled by this phenomenon. Could it have been an old inside wall-face at all? That seemed almost incredible, because it meant that the wall must have been thinned down at the angle of its junction with the Nave to a mere skin not much more than three or four inches thick! Soundings, however, confirmed our first impression. Under the plinth of the existing chancel-wall we found the footing of a much earlier wall constructed of infinitely better and harder mortar. This was all that remained of the greater part of the earliest chancel wall, and the later wall was built on the top of it. Our exposed plastered face was apparently a lucky survival of this earliest wall, for the lowest course of it shewed the same cutting-away of the angle. But why was this old wall so mutilated and then left with its surface plastered for permanent use? A glance back at the pier of the Chancel Arch brought illumination. This pier, it will be remembered, was also cut back and plastered; and the plaster was of the same kind. It was then that the conclusion became obvious. Both pier and wall-angle had been cut back as a kind of "squint" to give the worshippers in the Hudleston Chapel a clearer view of the Chancel. The line of vision along the pier and the wall-face ran directly to the centre of the East window, and must have given a much more extensive view of the Altar and Communion rails than we have ever enjoyed ourselves. This most interesting discovery leads us to certain clear conclusions. There must have been a Chancel wall of the same character as our modern one, before the Chancel Arch was built, and this wall must have been bonded into the East wall of the Nave instead of protruding blankly into the Church as it did when we used to know it. This means, of course, that the East wall of the Nave on that (the south) side came further across northwards, and that there must have been in old times a much smaller opening and a smaller arch. When the new Chancel Arch was built, it sprang from what had become the eastern pier of the new arcade; but this meant that the South wall of the Chancel was left "in the air," the angle of it blocking the view from the new Hudleston Chapel. It throws a light on the indifference (or daring) of our forefathers that they got over this difficulty by simply shearing away the face of the pier and the wall until they got the line of vision which they required. At any rate, it is a comfort to feel that we shall have, in the future, a better vision without the danger of instability which they seem to have ignored!

This report has already grown to much greater length than was intended, and we must bring it to an end. One problem which still awaits solution is that the floor level of the piers of the arcade (i.e., at its East and West ends) is about seven inches higher than the floor level of the bases of the pillars! This and the interesting problem of the Nave and Hudleston Chapel we must leave over for another time.   W. J. P. A.

The Millom Gazette – Friday, June 27th 1930

Image © Millom Heritage & Arts Centre

Holy Trinity Church, Chancel before and after Restoration

FORMER LOCAL LICENSEE INTERRED ON TWO CONTINENTS
BROUGHT FROM CANADA FOR INTERMENT

"In loving memory of Arthur beloved husband of Sarah Riding died April 11th 1930 aged 46 years. Also Sarah his wife died July 8th 1973 aged 88 years"

The mortal remains of Arthur Riding, of Moose Jaw, Saskatchewan, Canada, were interred on Tuesday last at the Holy Trinity Church, the Rev. H. J. W. Phythian-Adams conducting the service in a deeply impressive manor. Amongst the principal mourners present were: Mrs. S. A. Riding (widow), M. and Mrs. N. Riding (brother and sister-in-law), Mr. and Mrs. A. Riding (brother and sister-in-law), Mrs. F. Riding (sister-in-law), Miss Jackson (cousin), Mrs. E. Redhead (sister-in-law), Mr. and Mrs. James Redhead (brother and sister-in-law), Mr. and Mrs. Joseph Redhead (brother and sister-in-law), Mr. and Mrs. S. Redhead (brother and sister-in-law), Miss M. Redhead (niece), Mrs. Bains (cousin), Mrs. Butler (cousin), Mrs. Tyke (cousin), and Mrs. Huddleston (cousin). The remains were borne to their final resting place by Messrs. T. Wilson, J. Halliwell, J. Knipe, J. Livesey, W. Bickerstaffe, and H. Todd. Many floral tributes were laid upon the grave from relatives and friends.

Mr. Riding was well known in the locality and had, prior to emigrating to Canada, been the licensee of the John Bull Hotel, Silecroft, for a period of about 10 years. The deceased was a native of Leyland, Lancs., and was at one time employed at Messrs. Vickers, Barrow. Emigrating to Moose Jaw, Canada, some three years ago, Mr. Riding entered the employ of the American Brewery Co., and was held in high esteem by employers and fellow-employees. An accident to a hand, sustained whilst following his employment, was eventually the cause of his death in the hospital at Moose Jaw on Friday, April 11th.

The interment took place on Tuesday, the 15th April, at the Rosedale Cemetery, the service being conducted by the Rev. J. F. Butcher in the presence of a large gathering of relatives and friends. The body was raised from its resting place some two months later, and accompanied by Mrs. A. Riding and Miss M. Redhead, was conveyed by train across Canada. Owing to heavy rain which had fallen continuously for three weeks and resulted in the flooding of the Moose River, the Canadian Pacific Railway officials decided to switch the boat train on to the C.N.R. line, to avoid the flood; unfortunately this had the opposite effect, a train which had preceded the boat train ran headlong into the flooded river, several passengers being drowned, and but for the courage and endurance of the brakesman, who, though badly scalded, walked two miles along the line and succeeded in stopping the boat train on which Mrs. Riding and Miss M. Redhead were passengers, a terrible tragedy might have taken place. Before the line could be cleared a freight train following in the rear of the boat train crashed and six men were killed, the engineer and fireman later dying from their injuries. The whole of the night and following day, Wednesday, 25th June, was spent in the train at Caperon, Ont. The line was eventually cleared and the train switched back to the C.P.R. line, the intervening days being spent at the Place Viger Hotel, Montreal. The journey was continued on the Saturday, and eventually Quebec was reached five days late, some 46 passengers missing the boat "The Duchess of Richmond," which had delayed its sailing from Friday until Saturday morning. The party embarked on the "Empress of Australia," docking at Southampton after a seven days passage, and Mrs. A. Riding and her niece arrived at Millom on the mail train on Tuesday morning, July 8th, after a journey which took 14 days to complete.

Mr. J. Sharp, of Silecroft, accompanied by Mr. J. Redhead, motored to Southampton, having previously had an unnecessary journey to Liverpool to meet the boat the "Duchess of Richmond," and conveyed the body to Millom, arriving on Thursday afternoon. The funeral, as previously stated, took place on Tuesday.

The Millom Gazette – July 7th 1930

MILLOM PARISH CHURCH

Writing in the current issue of the Parish Church Magazine, the Vicar (Rev. W. J. Phythian-Adams) says:- I had been hoping by this time to be able to give you some idea of the date of our Re-consecration. I expect to know that within the next week, but it will come too late for insertion in the Magazine. The work is taking rather longer than was anticipated, but this is largely due to the re-roofing of the Nave and Hudleston Chapel. At the start we thought it would only be possible to do general repairs to these roofs and give them an interior coat of plaster, but as the work on the Chancel neared completion, and we were able to check up the costs to date, we found that for a comparatively small extra outlay we could strip the roofs entirely board, felt, and then re-slate them. I need not say what an advantage this would be, and I have no doubt that we shall easily raise the additional amount of £40 to £50. Meanwhile, there is nothing much to report, for "finds" have been disappointingly few. The most interesting is a curved fragment of stone, inscribed with the letters ANTEF, which, as they stand, mean nothing. It has, however, been suggested (I think correctly) that they are part of an old Roman inscription, and originally read "CURANTEF(LAVIO)." ["This building was erected] by the care of F[lavius]." That seems rather a lot to get out of five letters, but archaeologists can do that kind of thing, as I have reason to know myself! Of course, this inscription has no reference to the Church, nor need it have been meant for any building at Millom. I think it has possibly been brought here from some Roman site, such as Ravenglass or Hardknott. Anyhow, the stone is of great interest, and I have put it over the opening of the Piscina in the Chancel so that it may be certain of preservation.

The 'ANTEF' stone above the Piscina in the Chancel. Image © Bry Cooper

Another "find" consisted of two fragments of an old "Norse-type" cross which our local authority, Mr. F. Warriner, is inclined to date to the end of the 11th or the beginning of the 12th century. These fragments are now built into the outside of the north-east angle of the Chancel, and the larger, with its "Staffordshire knot" pattern, has already attracted considerable attention. The old cross-socket in the churchyard very possibly belonged to the Cross, which may have been the meeting place of the ancient Millom Fair.

Another discovery, which cannot be called a "find," may also be noticed, for it is at first sight very puzzling. The piers at the west and east ends of our central arcade were made originally for a higher floor-level than the present columns of the arcade. When the church is finished, you will notice that we have had to insert new masonry at their foot so as to bring them down to the level of the bases of the columns. I can only think of one explanation for this. There must have been an older and lower arcade before the existing one was built, and these piers must have been originally intended for that. They will then, in all probability, go back to the days of the first Hudlestons, and will be contemporary with our 13th or early 14th century Chancel arch. I believe that this curious discrepancy has not been noticed before, but it opens a new and hitherto unknown chapter in the history of the Old Church

The Millom Gazette – Friday, October 10th 1930

Millom Parish Church.

HISTORICAL EVENT AT MILLOM PARISH CHURCH
RE-OPENING AND DEDICATION

Millom's ancient and historic edifice, more popularly designated "The Old Church," which has during the past half-year been subjected to a most extensive scheme of restoration, was on Wednesday evening re-opened and solemnly dedicated by the Rt. Rev. the Lord Bishop of Carlisle. Briefly, the scheme has included complete reconstruction of the altar and chancel (from which latter all pews have been removed); the provision of a new organ and choir gallery (as a memorial to the men of the parish who made the supreme sacrifice in the Great War), which is in direct view of the chancel; the restoration of the ancient Hudleston chape; and the installation of electric lighting in place of gas.

A guard of honour was formed near the main entrance to the church by the 1st Millom Parish Church Boy Scouts.

The Bishop was accompanied by the Rural Dean, the Rev. J. W. Akam (Vicar of Seascale), Rev. W. J. Phythian-Adams (Vicar of Millom), Rev. A. S. Picton (curate), Rev. F. M. Beddow (Vicar of St. George's, Millom), Rev. W. S. Sherwen (Vicar of Thwaites), the following former clergy of Holy Trinity Parish: Vicars: Revs. R. S. G. Green (Vicar of Broughton-in-Furness), R. D. Ellwood (Vicar of St. Mary's, Carlisle), D. W. Irving (Vicar of St. Stephen's, Carlisle), and P. A. Stewart (Vicar of Scotby); Curates: Rev. W. S. Sykes (chaplain, General Hospital, Birkenhead, for the last 20 years), who succeeded the Rev. P. Ingledow as curate under the late Canon J. Irving; and the Rev. W. W. Farrer (Hesket-in-the-Forest).

Mr. Ferdinand Hudleston, of Hutton John, Penrith, a direct descendant of the one-time famous Hudleston family, of Millom, was also present at the service.

Mrs. D. Hawkrigg officiated at the organ, and the choir led in the singing of the hymns (A. & M. 166, 239, 320, 395, and 397).

The Bishop, in the course of his sermon (based on the 1st, 2nd and 12th verses of Psalm 84), said: Perhaps we none of us know rightly where that psalm was written, but certainly it was written a long way from Jerusalem, by a man who was in exile and looked back to the temple of worship which his forefathers had known, remembering all its glory and recalling all the power and influence it had once possessed; and as he looked back, if he knew anything of history, he could find clear indications of the power of worship and of its effect upon the national life of Israel; how the Jews were brought into contact with other things, how their commerce flourished and how their relations became extended to surrounding nations. The worship of Israel could not be separated from its history. The Psalmist could also have traced the slow growth of purer and more spiritual worship with more sincerity or more truth than when they had been separated from their temple and were looking back to it belonging.

And to-night, when we are offering our thanks and expressing our joy at the beautiful restoration of this church, we shall do right to think of the part the Church of England has played in the history of our nation. It came before the nation was, and through all the centuries has been the guardian of the English people; there has never been a time in which the Church has not pointed the way to righteousness and peace; the principles of Jesus Christ have been taught and lived in the churches and parishes of England through all English history, and the power of the Church of England is still manifested, most vividly, perhaps, in this very psalm. Doubtless he wrote it with thinking of the temple – the temple in all its glory – as it had grown from generation to generation in its magnificence to the glory of God; and yet when we hear and sing a psalm, maybe in this church on a summer evening, "the sparrow hath found her a house and the swallow a home," we perhaps remember some little country church where during our worship we have heard swallows twittering in the eaves or a bird fluttering in the rafters.

There is no parish which does not seem a little forlorn if it does not possess a church. We are right to remember this and the feeling it arouses – the deep instincts of our spiritual life, instincts which will never perish. There is something deeper and truer still I ought to say to you. There are many ways in which you can show your love for English churches. You can, if you wish, be quite sure that no national life can flourish except upon the basis of religion. Men will not sacrifice themselves for their nation unless the nation stands for some eternal cause; and there is no doubt about the usefulness, nay, the inevitable necessity, of religion if the nation is to be great – but religion does not exist in order to redound (sic.) to the greatness of nations. His Lordship added that in the building of churches, the development of architecture or the recovery of ideas and arts our ancestors had, or in the completion of any new artistic conception of secular beauty, the first thoughts which prompted the efforts made in these directions should be of God. There is an economic history which might perhaps be traced even in their own church. They could quite certainly be sure that the first church which was built here was built by the gifts and through the munificence of the great aristocracy under which the people were in Feudal dependence – and they could be grateful that the early builders of churches in England had brought the nation into contact with other nations, and the Church of England into allegiance with the great Church of Rome. Yet we must search for something deeper if we are in our day to justify religion, not because Christianity cares merely for the poor, or because there is in religion an appeal for charity and love. Neither the historical glory of the Church of England, nor what it has bestowed upon the poor, nor its influence upon the arts, nor its attempts to creates a higher civilisation – none of these reasons lie really at the heart of the real need for Church. We must turn from these reasons to the need for finding God, and here in this psalm there are some indications of that necessity. The psalmist who wrote it was one who knew trouble and had tasted the bitterness of captivity. When he speaks of the man who, trusting in God, passed through the vale of misery and used it for a well, and "the pools are filled with water," by some kind of prophetic inspiration he saw what lay at the heart of our religion.

They were, that night, not only to thank God for a church far more beautiful than any of them had ever known it; not merely to thank Him for the art which has made it glorious or the craftsmanship which has created some, at least, of its early history; not merely to thank God for something much better, or the possibility of seeing in their lifetime this church restored, with a sanctuary large and fitting and proper for the uses of a sanctuary; for the gallery for the choir at the west end (where all choirs used at one time to be, and where he would that all choirs in churches were); they would be able to sing together as they had never been able to sing before, and they would be able to face the altar (which was not possible previously for all members of the congregation).

They were to thank Him for the new opportunity afforded to them "for finding God here as perhaps you have never found Him, and for learning Sunday by Sunday to worship Him in spirit and in truth." "The real reason for the existence of any church is not that you can is not that you can take pride in its possession as a memorial of your parochial history; it is not that you should be reminded of the legacy of your greatness entrusted to you by your forefathers – Englishmen who have made England great. All these reasons are valuable, but beneath and beyond them all is the necessity for worshipping God in our time with our knowledge and with our opportunities. Lift up your hearts to Him, determining that by His Grace you will make better use of this ancient and historic church which has been given to you as a living temple of the Lord Almighty, into which you shall come to worship and from which you shall go out to do God's work in the world. That is the true reason for the restoration of any church, and the great task that lies before our generation is surely that we should make God live in our national and civic life as He ought to live. No appeal, however eloquent, will rouse hearts to take the Divine message, and no teaching, however careful, can ever accomplish the task of teaching children religion; it is God, and God alone, Who by His power gives that inspiration which makes our religion live.

Therefore, tonight, let us leave this church with that last thought. Our true thankfulness is not to be discovered in our pride, our gratification, or our sense of work well accomplished. It will be found in the daily services you will attend here, in your lives and in your actions, and I am certain, as you are certain, that God has blessed this pious work, and I am confident if we raise our hearts to Him He will bless our worship, inspire our prayers, and illuminate our thanksgiving, and by His power and inspiration we shall be better men and women through the restoration of this church.

The service was brought to a close with the singing of a hymn (during which a collection was taken for the Restoration Fund), and the pronouncement of the Blessing by the Bishop.

SOCIAL GATHERING

A largely-attended social gathering of parishioners was subsequently held in the Palac, tea and refreshments being served by lady members of the Parochial Church Council and congregation. The evening's arrangements included a most enjoyable programme of musical selections by Mr. T. Richards' orchestra.

A brief interval was set apart for speechmaking, the Vicar (the Rev. W. J. Phythian-Adams) expressing his sincere thanks to the Bishop, who despite his innumerable engagements, had so kindly come all the way to Millom to perform the dedications in the service just concluded. It was also a matter for the very greatest pleasure to the speaker to see a member of that historic family (the Hudlestons) present at the service, and it was a delight to them all to be able to welcome him at that evening's proceedings – (applause). Further, the Vicar intimated what a great happiness it afforded himself and his parishioners generally to have with them that night four former Vicars of the parish and two past curates – (applause). In later words of comprehensive thanks for invaluable work and co-operation in connection with the work of Restoration, the Vicar specially mentioned the Parochial Church Council, committees, subscribers, the ladies who had cleaned the church in readiness for the re-opening service, the architects, organ-builders, builders and contractors, foremen, and the happy band of workmen who had been engaged.

The Rev. R. S. G. Green, the oldest surviving former Vicar of Millom, expressed the very great pleasure it afforded both himself and Mrs. Green to be able to be with their old parishioners that day, and to see the completion of the really wonderful work of restoration of the Old Church. He was vicar of the parish for over nine years, and the main recollection that he had taken away with him was the extraordinary affection and attachment the people of this parish had for the old church. He congratulated the present Vicar, the Church Council, committees and helpers generally upon their united effort to complete this wonderful achievement in restoring the church to what it probably resembled some 300 years ago. No one had taken part in Millom in a similar service to the one held that evening, and no one could therefore have had precisely that kind of experience. It must be a matter for great congratulation and rejoicing amongst the people of the parish to know that their church, which had weathered the storms of 800 or 900 years, had been put into condition which would enable it to continue as the centre of beneficent work in the parish. He trusted that they would not only receive the benefits, but would hand on the church to the people who followed them with the same enthusiasm fir it as was shown by their forefathers, and that they would have the same cause to love it as their predecessors had done – (applause).

Mr. Rainey (builder) and Mr. Hicks (architect) responded to the words of thanks from the Vicar, the former describing the Rev. Adams as a most efficient and assiduous "clerk of works."

The Bishop said that in consideration of the fact that he had already spoken at some length at the church service, he hoped he might have been excused from speech-making at this later function – but Mr. Adams had insisted otherwise. He could think of no one further to whom thanks were due (and had not already been given) unless it was the ladies who had provided the very excellent coffee and refreshments that evening – (laughter and applause). He wished , however, to thank them in all sincerity, as he regarded that part of the proceedings as a continuation of the service in church. Mr. Adams had done very great work for them in Millom in securing the services of Mr. Hicks. The latter might know more about churches than he (the speaker), but he himself had no little knowledge of churches from perhaps a rather different point of view, which, however, he did not know whether he could quite explain. When entering a church it was to him as though he were going into a living presence. Churches were alive, and not "dead" things. One could go into a church and know whether it is "cold" or "chill," and know whether the fault attaches to the architect, clergyman, or even the congregation. There was "something different" about each church. He would say now that their church "lives" – lives more fully and in more representative degree for the parish than at any time previous in his knowledge, and there was not now that feeling that it had been "damaged." He would also like to say a word of thanks to the choir: sometimes an organ ruins a choir, but that evening they had had neither too much organ nor too much choir; it was "first-rate," and he thought that the music had been admirably given. Looking back over the times he had been to Millom, His Lordship said it had been a matter of real thankfulness and joy to him that this great work had been accomplished, and he assured his hearers that they had in Millom one of the most interesting parish churches in the diocese, restored not merely from an antiquarian point of view, but its old life had been recreated again. One thing further he wished to say about Mr. Phythian-Adams, and that was a word of tribute at the very large part he had played in bringing about one of the most admirable restorations in the diocese. The speaker had heard at first-hand what an excellent "clerk of works" their Vicar had proved himself, and he would now take the opportunity of asking him in public (he might only decline if asked privately) to become a member of the Advisory Council which dealt with such matters in the diocese.

The Restoration Scheme, including the new organ (£1,000) was estimated to cost £5,000, of which only about £600 remains to be raised. This sum does not include the High Altar and its furnishings, which have been presented at a cost of about £250.

Contracts for the work of restoration were fulfilled by:- Architects, Messrs. Hicks and Charlewood, Newcastle-upon-Tyne; Organ-builders, Messrs. Harrison and Harrison, Durham; Builders & contractors, Messrs. Rainey Bros., Barrow-in-Furness (painting, etc., Mr. W. Ramsay, Barrow-in-Furness); Electric 'secret' lighting, Messrs. C. H. Mauger, Newcastle-upon-Tyne; McClary pipeless central heating, agents: Messrs. T. F. Tyson and Sons, Ltd., Ulverston

The Millom Gazette – Friday, December 19th 1930

The Hudleston Chapel Holy Trinity Church, Millom

The Hudleston Chapel Holy Trinity Church, Millom

Holy Trinity Church, Millom

1931

MILLOM VICAR'S DIOCESAN APPOINTMENT

The work of the Rev. W. J. Phythian-Adams, Vicar of Holy Trinity Church, Millom, in connection with the restoration of that church, has had a sequel in his appointment to the Bishop of Carlisle's Advisory Council on church alterations.

Making the announcement, the Bishop says:- "The work which Mr. Adams, in conjunction with Mr. Hicks, the Newcastle architect, who had already helped us so greatly in the diocese, has accomplished in the restoration of Holy Trinity Church, Millom, is quite admirable in its careful and scrupulous preservation of all that was venerable in our ancient church and its re-construction of the original purpose and intention of the building for corporate worship and devotion.

I wish that more use were made of the Advisory Council. It exists in order to give advice and information to incumbents and church councils before faculties are applied for. Its most useful function is to suggest names of architects, craftsmen, and firms of established reputation among whom a choice may be made. It has no desire to dictate, but it is anxious to help and to give advice. And I think that Canon Saunders, the secretary, might save many parishes from disastrous mistakes if early application were made to him for information from the Council."

Comment on the re-opening of the church is made in the Carlilse "Diocesan Gazette" by Mr. Adams, who writes:-

"To all who value the Catholic heritage of the Church of England, an occasion like this must be a source of great inspiration and encouragement. For the first time since the Reformation this ancient church has won back the dignity and beauty which it once possessed, and has thus linked our generation with those faithful souls who built and adorned it long centuries ago. It was most fitting that at the service of dedication this thought should find a visible embodiment, and that a Hudleston, standing by the tombs of his ancestors, should see their chapel restored to its ancient use."

The Millom Gazette – Friday, January 9th 1931

PRAISE FOR MILLOM VICAR

COMPLETION OF £6,000 RESTORATION SCHEME

The Rev. W. J. Phythian-Adams, vicar of Holy Trinity, Millom, was congratulated by the annual meeting of the parochial church electors last evening, on his valuable work in connection with the restoration of the church, which has recently been completed at a cost of approximately £6,000, including a £1,000 organ, which is a memorial to parishioners who lost their lives in the war. The scheme was taken in hand several years ago, but had been considerably delayed.

The annual statement of accounts, submitted by the hon. Treasurer, Councillor W. S. Farren, showed that, although the church had been closed for six months while the restoration work was in progress, a debt balance of £71 7s. 7d. at the beginning of the year had been changed to a credit of £146 19s. 1d. at the end of December. About £129 of that amount was earmarked for further special requirements.

Lancashire Daily Post – January 22nd 1931

NEW VICAR OF MILLOM

We understand that the living of Holy Trinity, Millom, has been offered to and accepted by the Rev. M. M. Barlow, M.A., curate of St. Andrew's, Penrith. Mr. Barlow was educated at Rossall School, and later proceeded to Brasenose College, Oxford. After taking his degree, Mr. Barlow received theological instruction at the Clergy Training School (Westcote House, Cambridge). Ordained to the curacy of Stanwix by the Bishop of Carlisle in 1924, he went to Penrith as Canon Byard's assistant in 1927

The Millom Gazette – Friday, May 8th 1931

INDUCTION AT MILLOM PARISH CHURCH

The collation and induction of the Rev. M. M. Barlow, M.A., to the living of Holy Trinity, Millom, took place on Saturday last, before the Lord Bishop of the Diocese. The Rural Dean (Rev. J. W. Akam) acting as the Archdeacon's deputy, inducted the new Vicar, and the Rev. W. J. Phythian-Adams carried the Pastoral Staff as the Bishop's chaplain. Other clergy present were: Revs. F. M. Beddow (St. George's, Millom), W. S. Sherwen (Thwaites), W. L. Thomas (Bootle), C. B. How (Seathwaite), B. S. Simpson (Ulpha), and A. S. Picton (St. Luke's, Barrow).

The Millom Gazette – July 31st 1931

1932

NEW CARLISLE CANON
THE REV. W. PHYTHIAN-ADAMS APPOINTED

The Bishop of Carlisle has appointed the Rev. W. J. T. Phythian-Adams, M.A., to be a Canon Residentiary of Carlisle Cathedral. The new Canon has had a distinguished career. He was at Christ Church, Oxford, where he took a first-class in Lit. Hum. In 1911. Serving in the Great War, he was awarded the M.C. in 1917 and the D.S.O. in 1918. At the close of the war he studied at Cuddesden Theological College, Oxford until 1924. After holding a curacy at Wellingborough he became Vicar of Holy Trinity, Millom, where he remained until last year. For the past few months he has acted as Bishop's Messenger in the diocese of Carlisle

The Millom Gazette – Friday, February 26th 1932

CORRESPONDENCE
GRAND ORIENTAL BAZAAR.
(To the Editor of the 'Millom Gazette').

Sir, I would ask the courtesy of your columns to bring to the notice of your readers the Grand Oriental Bazaar to be held in the Palace, Market Square, next week, in aid of the Restoration Fund of the Old Church.

On Wednesday and Thursday, June 8th and 9th, a determined effort will be made to clear off a debt of about £70 and we are very anxious that next week should see the triumphant conclusion of an enterprise which has extended over a number of years.

This letter is by way of an appeal to all your readers to come to the aid of the Mother Church of Millom. There is no doubt whatever that the old churches of England are a source of inspiration to all, whether they belong to the Anglican Communion or not, and I am sure that everybody in Millom is proud to have such a beautiful church in their midst, or at any rate, not far from their midst!

Next week, an opportunity will be given to all of showing their thankfulness for what is one of the most beautiful churches in Cumberland. Its antiquity points not only to the love and devotion of generations long ago – but also and supremely – to the fact that these past generations realised the centrality of religion and built to the glory of God.

And we in this generation must not be unworthy of so goodly a heritage, but thankfully maintain that which has been handed down to us, so that in years to come it may be said of us that we instinctively knew the vital importance of the Christian Faith, and did all in our power on its behalf by securing for those who came after us a beautiful House of God.

Some of your readers, I know, live up at Ulpha, and to them also I would make a special appeal on behalf of their Mother Church. Those who live up the Duddon Valley are surrounded by the beauties of nature, and I would ask them also to consider the beauties of architecture and give thanks in a practical manner to the God who makes all lovely things and help others to build lovely things.

Lady Hutchinson from Ravenglass is kindly coming to open the Bazaar on the first day at 2.30 p.m., and A. R. Pennington, Esq., Hawthwaite How on the second day at the same hour.

Yours very truly, M. M. Barlow, The Vicarage, Millom. June 2nd 1932

The Millom Gazette – Friday, June 3rd 1932

```
MILLOM PARISH CHURCH.
           — GRAND —
    ORIENTAL BAZAAR
           — IN —
       THE PALACE, MILLOM,
              — ON —
WEDNESDAY & THURSDAY, JUNE 8th & 9th, 1932
       IN AID OF THE CHURCH RESTORATION FUND.
        1st Day.                    |         2nd Day.
The Bazaar will be Opened at 2-30 p.m. by | The Bazaar will be Opened at 2-30 p.m. by
    Lady Hutchinson.                |     A. R. Pennington, Esq.
STALLS—Provisions, Cakes, Fancy, China & Basket, Sweets & Ices
   Childrens Stall, Kirksanton Stall, The Hill Stall, Parish Church Stall.
SIDESHOWS.         TEAS PROVIDED both days.
                    ADMISSION:
1st DAY: 1/- up to 6 p.m.; 6d., 6 to 8 p.m. Children Half Price. 2nd DAY: 6d. Children Half Price.
     There will be a GRAND DANCE on THURSDAY at 9 p.m.
     (After the Bazaar closes).   ADMISSION   -   1/-.
```

The Millom Gazette – Friday, June 3rd 1932

MILLOM PARISH CHURCH EFFORT

GRAND ORIENTAL BAZAAR

MAGNIFICENT DECORATIVE SCHEME

The opening of an Oriental Bazaar held in the Palace Cinema during Wednesday and Thursday marked the culmination of many months of preparation on the part of the various organisations connected with Holy Trinity Church. The effort was an endeavour to raise funds whereby the debt incurred in the restoration of the historic Parish Church might be liquidated, and has been organised by a committee of enthusiastic and resourceful workers of the parish, of which the Vicar (Rev. M. M. Barlow) is chairman, Mr. H. G. Scott and Miss Jackson filling the offices of treasurer and secretary respectively.

WEDNESDAY

On entering the Palace, one was immediately transported in fancy to the glorious East, the land of golden domes and minarets. The fascinating atmosphere of an Eastern bazaar pervaded the whole building, the designers (Mr. and Mrs. C. Coade) and their willing band of workers having captured the true spirit of the East, and infused it into their work, with the result that one wandered in amazement through stalls of various kinds heavily laden with the work of many hands, whilst overhead towered the statley domes and minarets, decorated in most artistic manner with beautiful foliage and lighted with multi-coloured Chinese lanterns, which bore evidence to the artistry of the workers who participated in the decorating. Mr. and Mrs. Coade have in the past earned unstinted praise and admiration for their achievements in connection with similar efforts, but on this occasion they have undoubtedly excelled themselves in the matter of designing. The naturalness and beauty of the scene was added to by the brilliantly and charmingly costumed stall-holders.

The opening ceremony was performed by Lady Hutchinson, of Ravenglass, and she was supported by the Rev. M. M. Barlow (chairman) and Mr. G. H. Scott.

The Chairman, at the outset, said it had been agreed that punctuality was the secret of success, so that it behoved them to commence their opening ceremony punctually. Before introducing Lady Hutchinson, he wished to express his delight at seeing such a large gathering present, who would, he was sure, join with him in praise of the beautiful decorative work that had been done, and they congratulated the genius behind the scheme. They were there, he said, for two things, business and pleasure. The business was very serious, and embraced selling and buying, whereby they could make money to vanquish the odour of debt which surrounded them. He hoped the bazaar would raise at least £400; their debt was exactly £370, but he felt if they aimed at the very highest they would not be too disappointed if they failed. £300 of the sum required held a special significance for them, being the amount loaned them, free of interest, by his predecessor, Canon Phythian-Adams and Miss Adams, the remaining £70 being required to clear the debt. That is the real reason why we are here, coupled with the pleasure of a kind of family gathering. Mr. Barlow then introduced Lady Hutchinson, and asked her to declare the bazaar open.

Lady Hutchinson said that she had visited their church about ten days ago, and had been much impressed by its beauty. It was up to them to see that it was handed on to the next generation with that beauty unimpaired; it was a valuable link, not only in history of the historic castle, but also in the history of England, and it should be treasured as such. There had been cases of so-called restorations where the old building had been completely destroyed, but that was not so with their church. The work of the original builder had been most carefully preserved, and the actual beauty retained.

"Perhaps I had better talk a little about the bazaar," she added. "People always grumbled when bazaars were mentioned: What, another one!" "But there was something good about bazaars: people come and spend their money, and thus assist in raising the required sum. Bazaars also called for self-sacrifice and goodwill, and demanded the co-operation of the workers as well as remaining by far the most popular method adopted by churches and other organisations for raising funds." She had spent several years in the Near and Far East, India and Ceylon, therefore she had been interested more particularly in their Oriental Bazaar, and it was with great pleasure that she declared it open.

Mr. G. H. Scott proposed a vote of thanks to Lady Hutchinson for so willingly coming along to assist them in their task of clearing off the dept upon their beloved church and its associations which were so dear to them. The work of restoration had brought back the old spirit which it contained within its walls. Whilst they were thanking Lady Hutchinson, he thought they ought also to express their appreciation of all their former Vicar (Canon Phythian-Adams) and his sister had done for them in loaning them money and so spiritually restoring the old Church – (applause).

Amongst those present were: - Rev. F. M. Beddow (Vicar of St. George's) and Mrs. Beddow, Rev. J. Davidson (curate, St. Luke's) and Mrs. Davidson, Hon. Dorothy and the Hon. Elinor Cross, Mr. W. F. Sadler, C.C., and Mrs. Sadler, Rev. C. E. Last (curate, Holy Trinity), Messrs. W. D. Barratt, C.C., J.P., and F. G. Mills, J.P. and many others.

THURSDAY

The second day's opening ceremony was undertaken by Mr. A. R. Pennington, of Hawthwaite How, Broughton-in-Furness, and was attended by a large assembly, all of whom were unanimous in their admiration of the delightful decorative scheme. The proceedings were again presided over by the Vicar, who extended a cordial welcome to all present, many of whom he knew had attended the previous day's bazaar, and he thanked them for their support. He also thanked the numerous workers and stall holders for their work on the previous day, and their preparatory task for that day's function. He wished to remind them of the initial purpose of the effort, which was to wipe off the debt incurred by the restoration of their church, which was £370. He was very pleased to tell them that the takings and donations given privately amounted to £170, which was exceptionally good, and he hoped that by the end of that day to have not only equalled that sum but even surpass it – they aimed at £400, and he hoped they would not be disappointed. Mr. Pennington would be known to many of them as one who was keenly interested in Scouts and Rovers. It was rather a strange coincidence that both Lady Hutchinson and Mr. Pennington having held the important post of Chief Justice during his sojourn in the East. He had been in Millom many times, and often brought his friends to see the church, and it was with much pleasure that he called upon Mr. Pennington to declare the bazaar open.

Mr. A. R. Pennington confessed that he felt he was in rather a strange land – he was really a Lancashire lad. He had been in Millom a number of years ago on many occasions, but his activities had been confined to the football and cricket fields; however, during that time he had discovered that Millomites were all good sports, and nice to be amongst. Referring to the restoration of the church, Mr. Pennington said churches like theirs were rather chary about restoration. During the last century a number of churches had been "restored," and emerged from the operation considerably worse than before. That was ruthless restoration, no account having been taken of the beauty of the building and resembled patches on an old garment. With the church of Holy Trinity, however, the work has been done with a spirit of reverence; the person responsible had sat down and thought and got into the spirit of the church – the spirit and individuality of the men who built it. They were to be congratulated upon their beautiful church – it was one they ought to be proud of. He often had visitors at Broughton, and when they asked if there was anything they ought to see he always said "Yes, there's the Millom Parish Church." That was one reason why he was glad to assist to clear the debt of the church. Another reason was that he was at St. John's, Cambridge with their Vicar's father, and he had many happy memories of those days at college. "Your Vicar went to Oxford, but feel that is not an unforgiveable sin; you can feel sorry for him" – (laughter). Mr. Pennington said he had great pleasure in declaring the bazaar open.

A vote of thanks to Mr. Pennington was proposed by Mr. J. H. Jenkinson, who said it was very good of him to perform the opening ceremony.

This concluded the ceremony of the opening and the stalls were then besieged by buyers desirous of assisting in a practical manner the work for which the function was organised.

STALLS AND STALLHOLDERS

Parish Church Stall. – Mrs. Pixton, Miss Sykes, Mrs. Harrison, Mrs. Coward, Mrs. Sharp, Mrs. Burn, Mrs. Clarke, Mrs. Twiname, Mrs. Barton and Miss Coward.

Provisions. – Mrs. Prickett, Mrs. Sadler, Misses Watson, Coward, Allanson and Andrews.

Fancy Stall. – Mrs. Barratt, Miss Dawson, Miss Johnson, Miss Phythian-Adams and Mrs. Pratt.

Children's Stall. – Mrs. Young, Miss Singleton and Miss Park.

Cake Stall. – Mrs. A. Jones, Mrs. Riley and Miss Jackson.

Sweets. – Misses Scott, Graham, Hoyle, Prickett and Fox.

The Hill Stall. – Mrs. Preston, Mrs. Cartwright, Misses Storey, Coulter, Shaw, Cranke and Dobson, Messrs. Kitchin, Bertram and Dobson.

Kirksanton. – Misses Hudson, Park, Benn, Williamson, A. Wallbank, Sawrey, Mawson, Wallbank, Thompson and Crayston.

Men's Stall (crockery and basket). – Messrs. S. R. Barber, T. J. Whinray, E. Ellwood and T. Huddleston.

Side Shows. – G.S.M. J. Jenkinson, S.M. E. Nicholson, A.S.M. H. Riley, C.M. E. Holmes, A.C.M. I. Billing, P.L. N. Casson, P.L. H. Richardson, Rover Leader J. Mitchell, Rovers W. Bertram and E. Casson.

Bran Tub. – Misses Ivy Whitford and M. Coward.

An appetising tea was served, the following ladies presiding over the tables: Mrs. Jenkinson, Misses Atkinson, Shaw, Preston, Mesdames Gaitskell, Gardner, Farren, Fawcett, Davis, Wilson, Moore, Wall, Knowles and Satterthwaite, assisted by members of the Women's Bible Class: Mesdames Cooper, Steele, Chambers, Blamire, Woodend, Myers, Wilson, Fallows, Sharpe, Seward, Gibbs, Woodend, Ashburner and J. Crellin.

Music was provided on both afternoons by the following orchestra: Mrs. Hawkrigg, Messrs. T. Richards, T. Johns, F. Lorraine, E. Watson, E. Agnew, B. Moore and W. Williams.

THE DANCE

As a wind-up to the second day's proceedings, a well-attended dance was held, Mr. Usher's Band providing music in their usual efficient manner; the bandsmen were attired in Chinese costume, and added to the gaiety of the scene. Duties of M.C.'s were undertaken by Messrs. R. Davis, S. Burn, W. Jenkinson, J. Jenkinson and A. Ellwood, an enjoyable evening resulting. Refreshments were served by the ladies committee.

The Millom Gazette – Friday, June 10th 1932

REV. W. J. T. PHYTHIAN-ADAMS

The Rev. William John Telia Phythian-Adams was on Friday afternoon installed into the 1st Canonry of Carlisle Cathedral, in succession to Canon Hopkinson. The Bishop of Carlisle, the Dean of Carlisle, Archdeacon Campbell and Canon Boulton were present. The installation was performed by the Dean and Mr. A. N. Bowman, as Clerk to the Dean and Chapter, administered the oaths.

The Millom Gazette – Friday, June 17th 1932

REV. D. W. IRVING

The Rev. D. W. Irving, Vicar of St. Stephens, Carlisle, and formerly curate at Barrow-in-Furness and Vicar of Millom, has accepted a post as chaplain at Haifa, Palestine. He is one of the sons of the late Canon Irving, Hawkshead, and he entered Haifa with the British Troops during the war.

The Millom Gazette – Friday, September 30th 1932

1933

FORMER MILLOM VICAR MADE CHAPLAIN TO THE KING

The "London Gazette" states that Canon W. J. T. Phythian-Adams, Canon of Carlisle and Canon J. C. H. How, Canon and Rector of Liverpool, have been appointed chaplains to the King, in succession to the late Rev. W. J. Wickins and Canon C. S. Woodward, Bishop designate of Bristol respectively.

Canon Phythian-Adams was educated at Corpus Christi College, Oxford, where he graduated with honours. He was awarded the M.C. and D.S.O. during the war. Afterwards he attended Cuddleston College, and was ordained in 1924, becoming a priest the following year.

Canon Phythian-Adams, who became a canon of Carlisle last year, was formerly assistant director of the British School of Archaeology at Jerusalem and Keeper of the Museums to the Palestine (Government) Administration. He collaborated with Professor Garstang in archaeological excavations in Northern Syria, the Sudan and Palestine. He was ordained in 1925, and for four years (1927-31) was Vicar of Millom.

The Millom Gazette – March 10th 1933

1935

REV. M. M. BARLOW ACCEPTS LIVING OF CORBRIDGE

The Rev. M. M. Barlow, Vicar of Holy Trinity, Millom, and formerly curate of Penrith Parish Church, has been offered and has accepted the living of Corbridge-on-Tyne, in the diocese of Newcastle. The Dean and Chapter of Carlisle are patrons of the living of Corbridge.

Penrith Observer – Tuesday, June 4th 1935

REV. SAMUEL TAYLOR ACCEPTS LIVING OF MILLOM

Rev. Samuel Taylor, Vicar of Holy Innocents, Manchester, has accepted the living of Millom, vacant by the cession of the Rev. M. M. Barlow, who has been instituted to the living of Corbridge-on-Tyne. The Bishop of Carlisle is the patron.

Lancashire Daily Post – Friday, September 6th 1935

BARROW VICAR

MARRIED TO A FORMER SCHOOL TEACHER

The wedding took place at Millom yesterday of Miss Mary Marr, of Millom, and the Rev. A. S. Picton, vicar of St. Luke's, Barrow, formerly a curate at Millom. The officiating clergyman was Canon Phythian-

Adams, of Carlisle, who was vicar of Holy Trinity, Millom, while the Rev. A. S. Picton was curate. Other clergy present were the Rev. H. Battye, vicar of St. Catherine's, Burnley, best man; Rev. W. Rhodes, of Leeds (formerly curate of St. Luke's, Barrow); Rev. J. C. Longbottom, of Heckmondwike Rev. W. Prest, curate-in-charge of Holy Trinity, Millom. The latter acted as organist.

The bride was given away by her father and she wore white satin beaute, with wreath and veil. She also carried a sheaf of Madonna lilies. There were three bridesmaids.

The bride was formerly a teacher at Egremont and Arlecdon, near Whitehaven.

Lancashire Daily Post – Wednesday, September 25th 1935

1956

Image © Bry Cooper

The marriage of Edward Barry Cooper, Patternmaker at Millom Ironworks, to Gladys Waugh at Holy Trinity Church, Millom on Saturday, September 15th 1956

1958

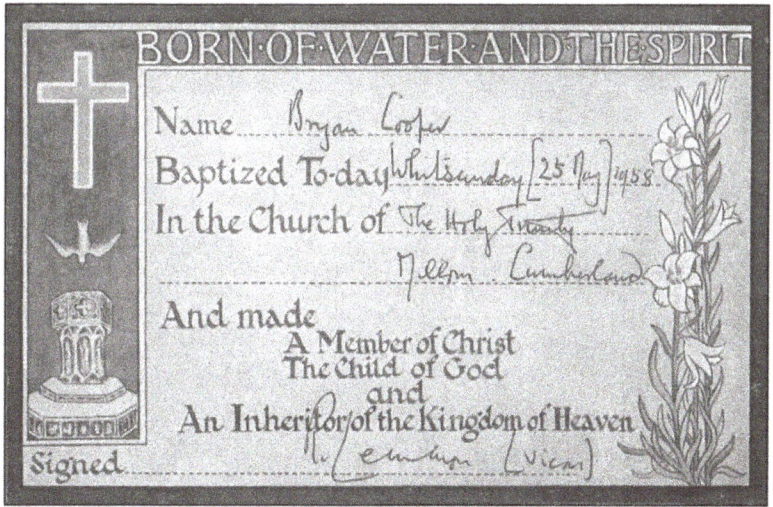

Image © Bry Cooper

The baptism of Bryan Cooper at Holy Trinity Church, Millom on Sunday, May 25th 1958

www.ingramcontent.com/pod-product-compliance
Lightning Source LLC
Chambersburg PA
CBHW042019090526
44590CB00029B/4334